SHARE the Music

McGRAW-HILL

AUTHORS

Judy Bond,
Coordinating Author

René Boyer-White

Margaret Campbelle-duGard

Marilyn Copeland Davidson,
Coordinating Author

Robert de Frece

Mary Goetze,
Coordinating Author

Doug Goodkin

Betsy M. Henderson

Michael Jothen

Carol King

Vincent P. Lawrence,
Coordinating Author

Nancy L. T. Miller

Ivy Rawlins

Susan Snyder,
Coordinating Author

McGraw-Hill
School Division

New York   Farmington

ACKNOWLEDGMENTS

Grateful acknowledgment is given to the following authors, composers, and publishers. Every effort has been made to trace the ownership of all copyrighted material and to secure the necessary permissions to reprint these selections. In the case of some selections for which acknowledgment is not given, extensive research has failed to locate the copyright holders.

Abingdon Press for *Thanksgiving* from CHERRY STONES! GARDEN SWINGS! by Ivy O. Eastwick. Copyright © 1962 by Abingdon Press. Used by permission.

ACUM Ltd. for *Feast of Light* by Sarah Levy-Tanai and Emanuel Amiran (Pugachov). © by the Authors, ACUM ISRAEL.

Alfred Publishing Co., Inc. for *When the Flag Goes By* by Lynn Freeman Olson from IT'S TIME FOR MUSIC. Copyright © 1985 by Alfred Publishing Co., Inc. Used by Permission of the Publisher. All Rights Reserved.

Bess Press for *Ku'u i'a* from PAI KA LEO. Copyright © Bess Press, Honolulu, HI.

Margaret Campbelle-duGard for *Make Up a Rhyme*, collected by Marjorie H. Campbelle. Copyright © 1979 Margaret Campbelle-duGard.

Canyon Records for *Honoring Song to Mt. McKinley (Athabascan Song)* from the album WALK IN BEAUTY, MY CHILDREN by the Bala Sinem Choir, courtesy Canyon Records, Phoenix, Arizona.

Cherry Lane Music Publishing Company, Inc. for *Goin' to the Zoo* by Tom Paxton. © Copyright 1961, Renewed 1989 Cherry Lane Music Publishing Company, Inc. This Arrangement © Copyright 1994 Cherry Lane Music Publishing Company, Inc. For *The Thing That Isn't There* by Tom Paxton. © Copyright 1987 Pax Music. This Arrangement © 1994 Pax Music.

Children's Better Health Institute for *In Memory* by Ericka Northrop from JACK & JILL, copyright © 1989 by Children's Better Health Institute, Benjamin Franklin Literary & Medical Society, Inc., Indianapolis, IN. Used by permission.

CPP/Belwin, Inc. for *Circus!; Song Time;* and *Springtime* by Lynn Freeman Olson from SONGS FOR OUR SMALL WORLD by Lynn Freeman Olson and Georgia Garlid. Copyright © 1986 by BELWIN MILLS PUBLISHING CORP., c/o CPP/BELWIN, INC., Miami, FL 33014. International Copyright Secured. Made in USA. All Rights Reserved. For *You Are My Sunshine* by J. Davis & C. Mitchell. © 1940 (Copyright Renewed) by PEER INTERNATIONAL CORPORATION. International Copyright Secured.

All Rights Reserved Including the Right of Public Performance For Profit. Controlled in Australia and New Zealand by LLLAN & CO. PTY. LTD., Melbourne. Controlled in the Philippines by Southern Music Publishing Co. (Australia) Pty. Ltd.

Randy DeLelles for *A Turkey Named Bert* by Randy DeLelles. © Randy DeLelles.

Katherine Dent for *When You Send a Valentine*, words by Mildred J. Hill, from Emilie Poulsson's HOLIDAY SONGS (published by Milton Bradley Company, Springfield, MA 01101), used by permission of Mrs. Katherine Dent.

Ell-Bern Publishing Company for *Pole, Pole*, words and music by Ella Jenkins, Ell-Bern Publishing Company, ASCAP.

European American for *Two Little Sausages* from MUSIC FOR CHILDREN; ORFF-SCHULWERK, Volume 2, American Edition. Copyright © 1977 by Schott Music Corporation. All Rights Reserved. Used by permission of European American Music Distributors Corporation, sole U.S. and Canadian agent for Schott Music Corporation.

Miriam B. Factora for *Sasara Ang Bulaklak* from MUSICAL FOLK GAMES OF MANILA (PHILIPPINES). Copyright © 1989 by Miriam B. Factora, Manila, Philippines.

Frank Music Corp. and Meredith Willson Music for *Seventy Six Trombones* from Meredith Willson's "The Music Man" by Meredith Willson. © 1957 (Renewed) FRANK MUSIC CORP. and MEREDITH WILLSON MUSIC. All Rights Reserved. Used by Permission.

Theresa Fulbright for *Martin Luther King* by Theresa Fulbright. Copyright 1973 by Theresa Fulbright.

Mary Ann Hall for *Take a Bite of Music* by Mary Ann Hall. © Mary Ann Hall's MUSIC FOR CHILDREN from TAKE A BITE OF MUSIC, IT'S YUMMY by Mary Ann Hall, 1986.

Hap-Pal Music Inc. for *Clickety Clack* by Hap Palmer and Martha Cheney. © 1976 Hap-Pal Music Inc.

HarperCollins Publishers, Inc. for *Scene* from RIVER WINDING by Charlotte Zolotow. Text copyright © 1970 by Charlotte Zolotow.

continued on page 373

McGraw-Hill School Division
A Division of The McGraw-Hill Companies

1998 Impression

Copyright © 1995 Macmillan/McGraw-Hill School Publishing Company

McGraw-Hill School Division
1221 Avenue of the Americas
New York, New York 10020

Printed in the United States of America
ISBN 0-02-295051-6 / 2

5 6 7 8 9 071 99 98 97

SPECIAL CONTRIBUTORS

Contributing Writer
Janet McMillion

Consultant Writers
Teri Burdette, Signing
Brian Burnett, Movement
Robert Duke, Assessment
Joan Gregoryk, Vocal Development/
  Choral
Judith Jellison, Special Learners/
  Assessment
Jacque Schrader, Movement
Kathy B. Sorensen, International Phonetic
  Alphabet
Mollie Tower, Listening

Consultants
Lisa DeLorenzo, Critical Thinking
Nancy Ferguson, Jazz/Improvisation
Judith Nayer, Poetry
Marta Sanchez, Dalcroze
Mollie Tower, Reviewer
Robyn Turner, Fine Arts

Multicultural Consultants
Judith Cook Tucker
JaFran Jones
Oscar Muñoz
Marta Sanchez
Edwin J. Schupman, Jr., of ORBIS
  Associates
Mary Shamrock
Kathy B. Sorensen

Multicultural Advisors
Shailaja Akkapeddi (Hindi), Edna Alba
(Ladino), Gregory Amobi (Ibu), Thomas
Appiah (Ga, Twi, Fanti), Deven Asay
(Russian), Vera Auman (Russian, Ukrainian),
David Azman (Hebrew), Lissa Bangeter
(Portuguese), Britt Marie Barnes (Swedish),
Dr. Mark Bell (French), Brad Ahawanrathe
Bonaparte (Mohawk), Chhanda Chakroborti
(Hindi), Ninthalangsonk Chanthasen
(Laotian), Julius Chavez (Navajo), Lin-Rong
Chen (Mandarin), Anna Cheng (Mandarin),
Rushen Chi (Mandarin), T. L. Chi (Mandarin),
Michelle Chingwa (Ottowa), Hoon Choi
(Korean), James Comarell (Greek), Lynn
DePaula (Portuguese), Ketan Dholakia
(Gujarati), Richard O. Effiong (Nigerian),
Nayereh Fallahi (Persian), Angela Fields
(Hopi, Chemehuevi), Gary Fields (Lakota,

Cree), Siri Veslemoy Fluge (Norwegian),
Katalin Forrai (Hungarian), Renee Galagos
(Swedish), Linda Goodman, Judith A. Gray,
Savyasachi Gupta (Marati), Elizabeth Haile
(Shinnecock), Mary Harouny (Persian),
Charlotte Heth (Cherokee), Tim Hunt
(Vietnamese), Marcela Janko (Czech), Raili
Jeffrey (Finnish), Rita Jensen (Danish), Teddy
Kaiahura (Swahili), Gueen Kalaw (Tagalog),
Merehau Kamai (Tahitian), Richard Keeling,
Masanori Kimura (Japanese), Chikahide
Komura (Japanese), Saul Korewa (Hebrew),
Jagadishwar Kota (Tamil), Sokun Koy
(Cambodian), Craig Kurumada (Balkan),
Cindy Trong Le (Vietnamese), Dongchoon Lee
(Korean), Young-Jing Lee (Korean), Nomi Lob
(Hebrew), Sam Loeng (Mandarin, Malay),
Georgia Magpie (Comanche), Mladen Marič
(Croatian), Kuinise Matagi (Samoan), Hiromi
Matsushita (Japanese), Jackie Maynard
(Hawaiian), David McAllester, Mike
Kanathohare McDonald (Mohawk),
Khumbulani Mdlefshe (Zulu), Martin Mkize
(Xhosa), David Montgomery (Turkish), Kazadi
Big Musungayi (Swahili), Professor Akiya
Nakamara (Japanese), Edwin Napia (Maori),
Hang Nguyen (Vietnamese), Richard Nielsen
(Danish), Wil Numkena (Hopi), Eva Ochoa
(Spanish), Drora Oren (Hebrew), Jackie
Osherow (Yiddish), Mavis Oswald (Russian),
Dr. Dil Parkinson (Arabic), Kenny Tahawisoren
Perkins (Mohawk), Alvin Petersen (Sotho),
Phay Phan (Cambodian), Charlie Phim
(Cambodian), Aroha Price (Maori), Marg Puiri
(Samoan), John Rainer (Taos Pueblo, Creek),
Lillian Rainer (Taos Pueblo, Creek, Apache),
Winton Ria (Maori), Arnold Richardson
(Haliwa-Saponi), Thea Roscher (German),
Dr. Wayne Sabey (Japanese), Regine Saintil
(Bamboula Creole), Luci Scherzer (German),
Ken Sekaquaptewa (Hopi), Samouen Seng
(Cambodian), Pei Shin (Mandarin), Dr. Larry
Shumway (Japanese), Gwen Shunatona
(Pawnee, Otoe, Potawatomi), Ernest Siva
(Cahuilla, Serrano [Maringa´]), Ben Snowball
(Inuit), Dr. Michelle Stott (German), Keiko
Tanefuji (Japanese), James Taylor
(Portuguese), Shiu-wai Tong (Mandarin),
Tom Toronto (Lao, Thai), Lynn Tran
(Vietnamese), Gulavadee Vaz (Thai), Chen
Ying Wang (Taiwanese), Masakazu Watabe
(Japanese), Freddy Wheeler (Navajo), Keith
Yackeyonny (Comanche), Liming Yang
(Mandarin), Edgar Zurita (Andean)

CONTENTS

Music Is Mine to Share

from **The Way to Start a Day**

The way to make a song is this—
   Don't try to think what words to use
   until you're standing
   alone.
   When you feel the sun
   you'll feel the song too.

Just sing it.

—*Byrd Baylor*

FIND THE STEADY BEAT

Have you ever made up words to sing? Songs can be about lots of things. Singing is a great way to start your day!

TAP each sun to keep the steady beat.

Song Time

Words and Music by Lynn Freeman Olson

1. Now for a song time, Hope we sing a long time,
2. Day song or night song, Heav-y song or light song,

When we sing there's mu-sic all a-round!
Tunes that take us trav-el-ing a-way!

We'll find a way now, We can sing and play now
Dark song or bright song, We will find the right song

Make a won-der-ful sound!
For a mu-si-cal day!

FIND the words for these pictures in "Song Time."

A NAME GAME

You can say your name
to a steady beat.

PAT and **CLAP** the
steady beat as you play
"Say Your Name."

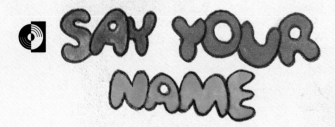

SAY YOUR NAME

Say   your   name and   when you   do

We   will   say   it   back to   you.

Rosa   Nashoba   Ann

ROBERT   John

Some names mean
special things.
Do you know what your
name means?

Different Ways

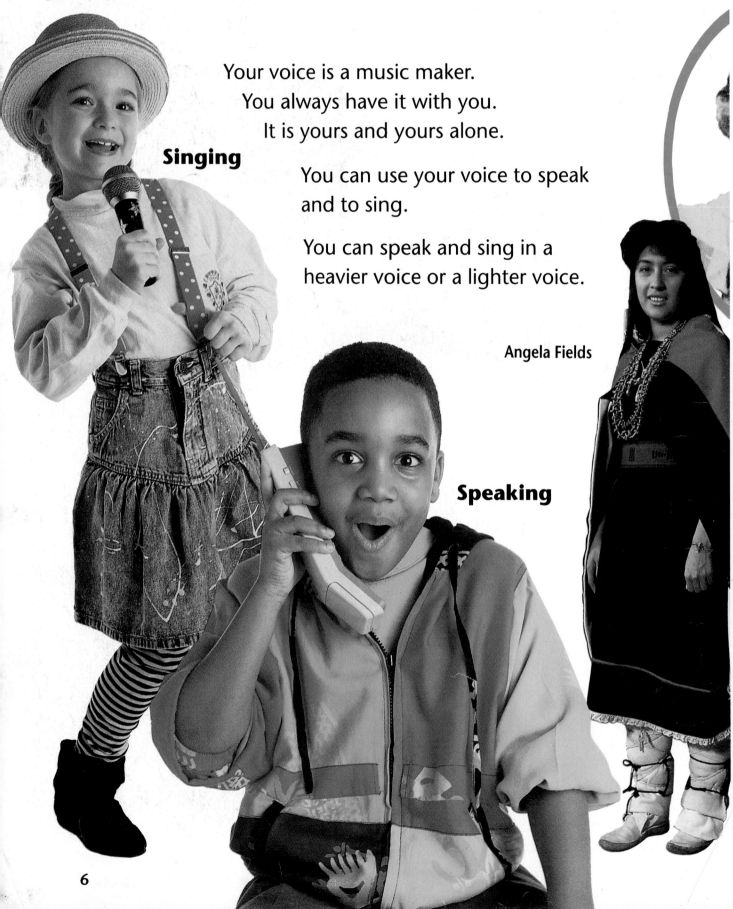

Singing

Your voice is a music maker.
You always have it with you.
It is yours and yours alone.

You can use your voice to speak
and to sing.

You can speak and sing in a
heavier voice or a lighter voice.

Angela Fields

Speaking

6

to Use Your Voice

Princess Elizabeth

Kathleen Battle

Bobby McFerrin

Martin Luther King, Jr.

Peking Opera Singer

🎵 LISTENING

Voices Around the World

💿 **LISTEN** to the different ways people use their voices. Then try some out!

Use a heavier voice and a lighter voice. Say the words to "Song Time." Then sing the song.

THINK IT THROUGH

How does a lighter voice sound different than a heavier voice?

LEARN this song from Ghana. Notice how the singers use their voices.

Thomas Appiah

Children in Ghana learn the movements to
"Kye Kye Kule" from older boys and girls.

KYE KYE KULE

Akan Call-and-Response Song

Leader   *Group*

Vocables: **Kye kye ku - le,** **(Kye kye ku - le,)**

Leader   *Group*

Kye kye ko - fi nsa, **(Kye kye ko - fi nsa,)**

Leader   *Group*

Ko - fi nsa lan - ga, **(Ko - fi nsa lan - ga,)**

Leader   *Group*

Ka - ka shi lan - ga, **(Ka - ka shi lan - ga,)**

Leader   *Group*

Kum a - den - de, **(Kum a - den - de,)**

All

Kum a - den - de, Hey!

HIDE AND SING

PLAY this hiding game.

One person leaves the circle.
Guess who is missing.

Here We Sit

American Singing Game

Here we sit in a ring.
Close your eyes now while we sing.
One of us will go and hide.
Guess who made that space so wide!

WHICH PITCH?

You can use your voice to make
sounds that are higher or lower.
Pitch is how high or low a sound is.

These shells show higher and lower pitches.

POINT **to a shell that shows higher.**

POINT **to a shell that shows lower.**

How are the shells like the first six
pitches of "Here We Sit"?

Higher

Lower

SHOW **higher and lower**
with your hands.

Fast, Slow
GO BEAT GO!

Play a new game to share with friends.

Head and Shoulders, Baby

African American Street Game
As Sung by René Boyer-White

1. Head and shoul-ders, ba - by, } one, two, three.
2. Knee and an - kle, ba - by, } one, two, three.

Head and shoul-ders, ba - by, } one, two, three.
Knee and an - kle, ba - by, } one, two, three.

Head and shoul-ders, head and shoul-ders, head and shoul-ders, ba-by,
Knee and an - kle, knee and an - kle, knee and an - kle, ba-by,

one, two, three.

3. Milk the cow, . . .   4. Throw the ball, . . .

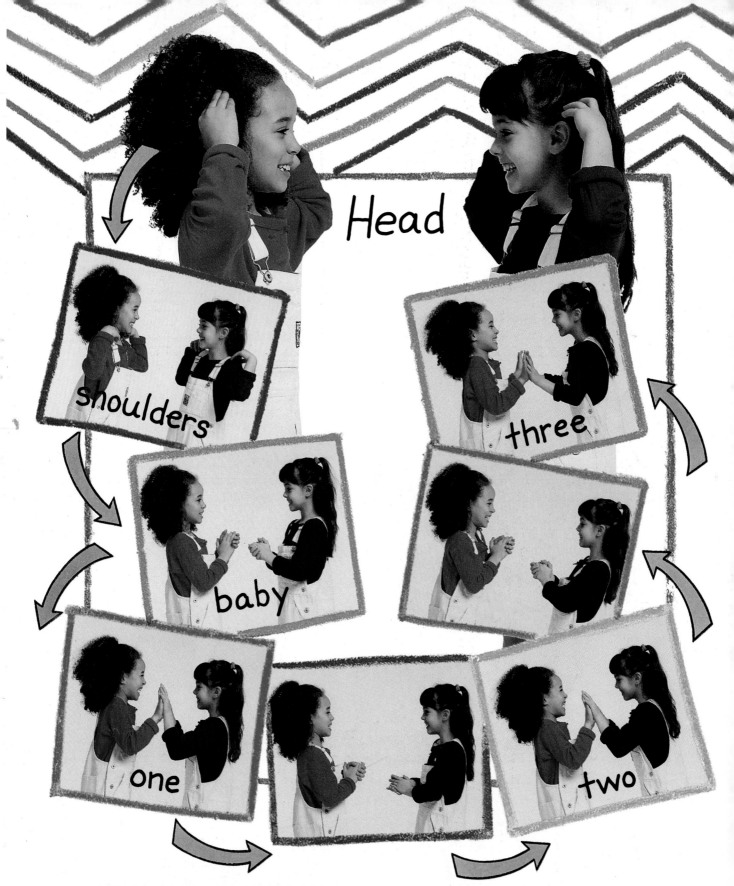

Head

shoulders

baby

three

one

two

THINK IT THROUGH

Compare "Kye Kye Kule" to "Head and Shoulders,
Baby." How are they the same? Different?

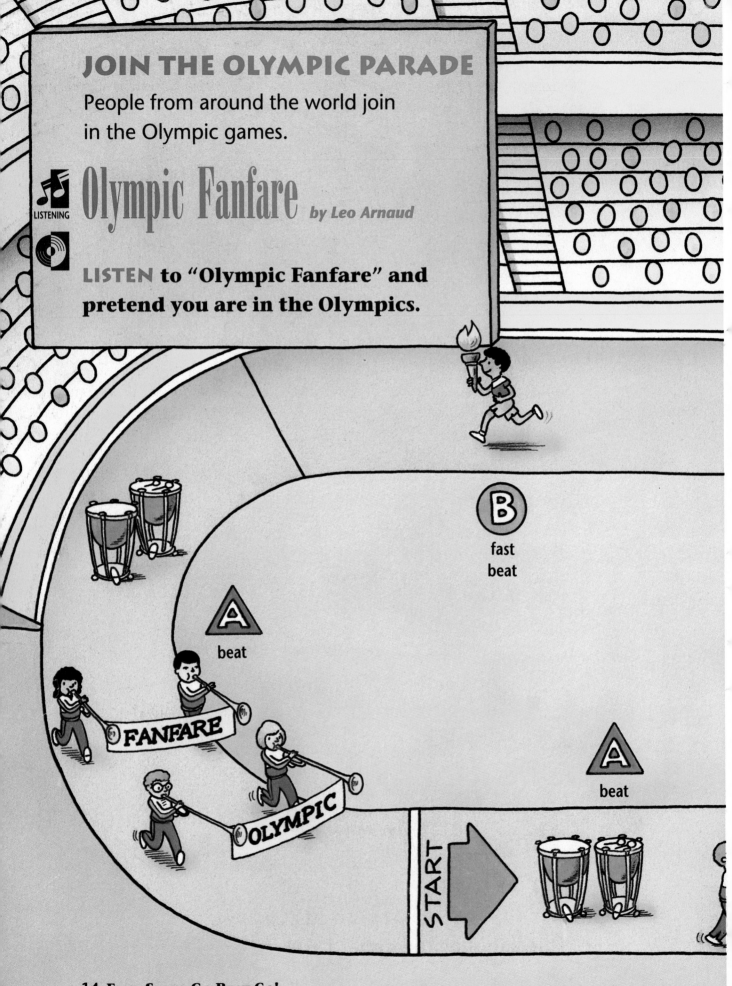

JOIN THE OLYMPIC PARADE

People from around the world join in the Olympic games.

LISTENING

Olympic Fanfare *by Leo Arnaud*

LISTEN to "Olympic Fanfare" and pretend you are in the Olympics.

LISTENING MAP *Follow the Olympic players. Notice when the beat gets faster or slower.*

C slow beat

B fast beat

FANFARE

OLYMPIC

Making RHYTHM TOGETHER

Sometimes sharing a song with a friend makes it more fun!

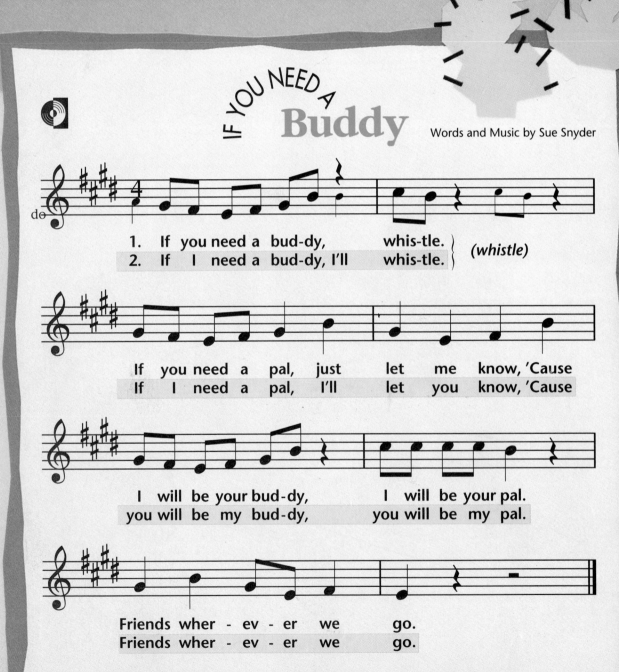

IF YOU NEED A Buddy

Words and Music by Sue Snyder

1. If you need a bud-dy,   whis-tle. } *(whistle)*
2. If I need a bud-dy, I'll   whis-tle. }

If you need a pal, just   let me   know, 'Cause
If I need a pal, I'll   let you   know, 'Cause

I will be your bud-dy,   I will be your pal.
you will be my bud-dy,   you will be my pal.

Friends wher - ev - er   we   go.
Friends wher - ev - er   we   go.

16

NOTES FOR LONG AND SHORT SOUNDS

In music, we can use this **note** to stand for one sound to a beat.

We can use these notes to stand for two shorter sounds to a beat.

WHAT IS RHYTHM?

Long and short sounds make **rhythm**.
You can read rhythm using these pictures.

SAY *buddies* **for two friends standing together.**

SAY *pal* **for one friend standing alone.**

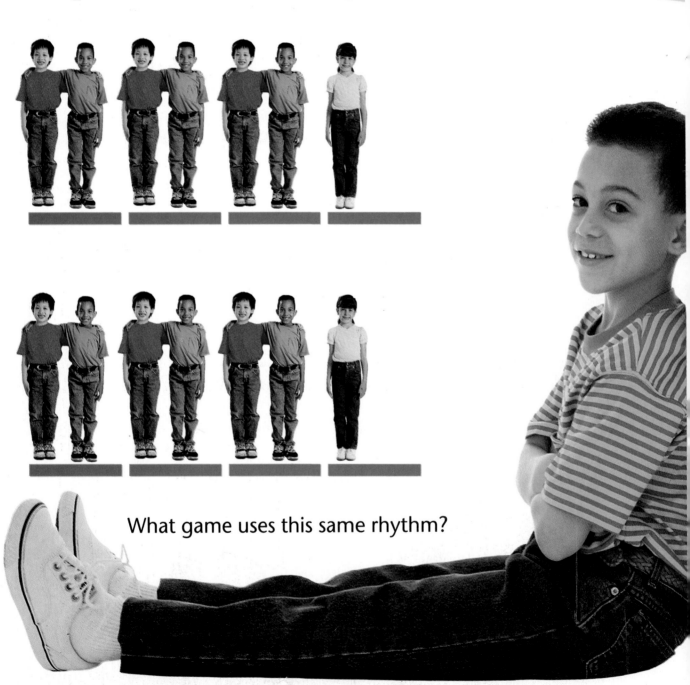

What game uses this same rhythm?

READ A RHYTHM

You just read a rhythm using pictures.

READ the same rhythm using notes.

Say *buddies* for ♫
Say *pal* for ♩

USE instruments to play this game.

Play Your Name

Play your name and when you do,

We will play it back to you.

UP and DOWN Sounds

Listen for *honk honk rattle rattle rattle crash beep beep*! Find these words in the song.

POINT to the cars to show how the pitches move in the first line.

I Have a Car

American Camp Song

I have a car, it's made of tin.

No - bod - y knows what shape it's in.

It has four wheels and a rum - ble seat.

Hear us chug - ging down the street.

Honk honk rat - tle rat - tle rat - tle crash beep beep.

Honk honk rat - tle rat - tle rat - tle crash beep beep.

Honk honk rat - tle rat - tle rat - tle crash beep beep.

Honk honk.

"Model T on the Farm " by Norman Rockwell ca. 1951-1952 The Henry Ford Museum and Greenfield Village.

MODEL T ON THE FARM BY NORMAN ROCKWELL

How is this car different from others you have seen?

Note heads show how high or low pitches are. They are written on lines and spaces called a **staff.**

Note heads can be around lines or in spaces. These note heads are around lines.

These note heads are in spaces.

TELL if these note heads are around lines or in spaces.

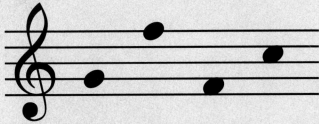

How can you tell which note head is highest? Lowest?

YOU CAN READ *MI* AND *SO*

Mi and **so** are pitch names.
Mi is always lower than *so*.

Look at *mi* and *so*. Are they
around lines or in spaces? You can
use what you know to read music!

READ the pitches in "Here We
Sit" by singing *mi* and *so*.
Then sing the song with
words.

Here We Sit

American Singing Game

Here we sit in a ring.   Close your eyes now while we sing.

One of us will go and hide.   Guess who made that space so wide.

A NEW PITCH NAMED *LA*

These cars show the first line of "I Have a Car."
Find *mi* and *so*. Find the pitch you do not know.

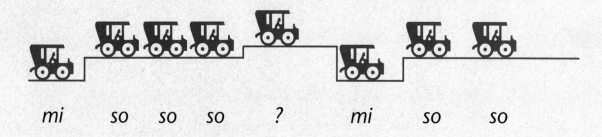

mi   so   so   so   ?   mi   so   so

The new pitch is **la.**

READ the pitches for the first line of
"I Have a Car."

     Sing *mi so* or *la* for each pitch.

La is around a line in this song.
So and *mi* are in spaces.

When *mi* and *so* are in spaces,
la will always be around a line.

You can read the pitches in this song.
So and *mi* are in spaces.

Where do you think *la* will be?

SING the pitch names.
Then sing the words.

BOUNCE HIGH
BOUNCE LOW

American Singing Game

la—so
mi→

Bounce high,   Bounce low,

Bounce the ball to   Shi - loh!

PLAY a bouncing game.

Pat the Beat, Clap the Rhythm

Each bar shows a beat.
PAT once for each beat.

The notes show the rhythm.
CLAP the rhythm.

What song do you know that has this rhythm?

Buddies and pals can play this Mexican game.

READ the rhythm.
Say *stir* for ♩
Say *bate* for ♫

Bate means "to stir very fast."

BATE BATE

Mexican Game

Spanish: **Ba** - te, ba - te, cho - co - la - te,

Con ar - roz y con to - ma - te.

LISTEN and LOOK

You know how to read pitches.
Can you hear what you see?

Listen to each pitch.

POINT to the pitch you hear on the staff below.

mi   so   la

Listen to these patterns.

POINT to the pattern you hear.

Spotlight on Anna Rubin

When Anna Rubin was a child, she thought that only very special people could write music. One day she tried it. It was easy and fun to do! Now she tells her students that anyone can write music, even if they only know one note!

Ms. Rubin used the idea of the wind when she wrote "Breezes." She wanted to show how a breeze might sound if it were music.

 Breezes *by Anna Rubin*
LISTENING

 LISTEN to "Breezes." *Take a walk through one of the pictures. Put the beat in your feet as you walk.*

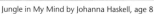
Jungle in My Mind by Johanna Haskell, age 8

USE *mi so* and *la* to sing about something you saw that you liked.

Montezuma's Head by Anna Althea Hills, Courtesy of the Maxwell Galleries, San Francisco

What did you see on your walk?

"Le Village en fête" by Miguel Vivancos, Musée National D'Art Moderne, Centre National d'Art et de Culture Georges Pompidou

Choose a
Way to Play

Instruments add to the fun of making music! You can use them to play beat and rhythm patterns.

CHOOSE an instrument and try different ways to play it. Decide on the way you like best.

PLAY along with "Bate, bate."

maracas güiro jingle bells tambourine

rhythm sticks claves wood block slit drum

hand drums bongos

cowbell hanging cymbal finger cymbals triangle

You can play pitches on some instruments.

POINT to *mi so* and *la.*

PLAY "Bounce High, Bounce Low."

xylophone

mi	so	la
F#	A	B

Which instruments can play *mi so* and *la*?

Which ones cannot play *mi so* and *la*?

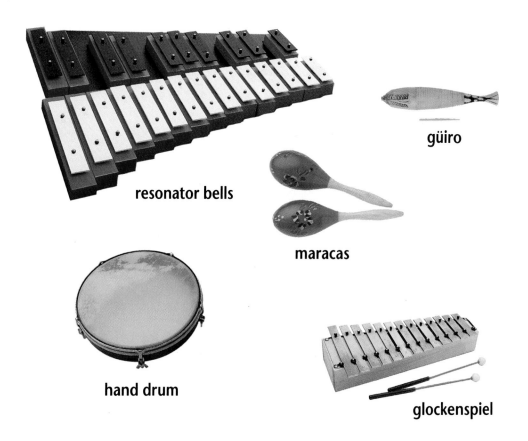

resonator bells

güiro

maracas

hand drum

glockenspiel

**CHOOSE rhythm instruments
to play with "I Have a Car." Use
different sounds for these words:**

Beep
Beep

Honk
Honk

Rattle Rattle
Rattle

CRASH

SING the song and play along.

FUN WITH FRIENDS

It's a beautiful day to play with friends!

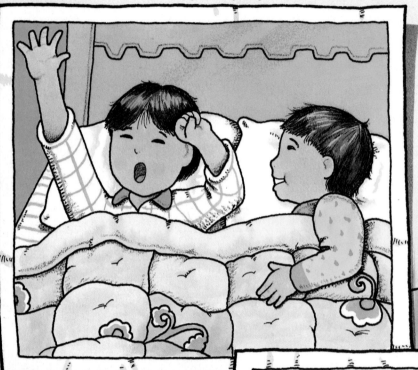

It's time to get up! What sounds that have no steady beat do you hear in the morning?

It's time for a song! Tap with the steady beat as you sing.

Buddies and pals can share this song. Who makes one sound on a beat? Who makes two?

Find *mi so* and *la*.

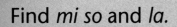

Sing a song about a funny car.

CHECK IT OUT

1. How would you move to this music?

   a. With a steady beat

   b. With no steady beat

2. Which rhythm do you hear?

   a.

   b.

   c.

3. Choose the pitches you hear.

   a.

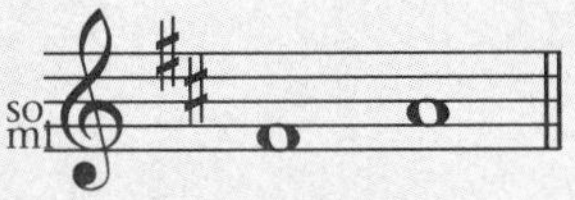

   b.

   c.

4. Which melody do you hear?

   a.

   b.

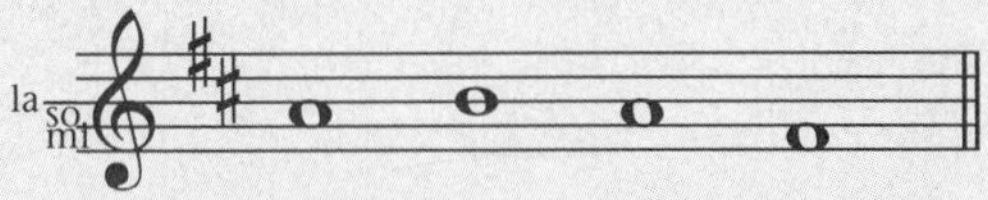

   c.

CREATE

MAKE UP your own rhythm using ♩ and ♫

Say and clap your rhythm.
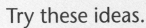
Say *pal* for ♩
Say *bud-dies* for ♫

BUDDIES! PALS!

Try these ideas.
Play your rhythm on an instrument.
Make up a melody for your rhythm.
Use *mi so* and *la.*
Add words to your rhythm.
Play your rhythm for the class.

Share

Think of something that you like about music
class. Choose a way to show a friend what
you like.

 Write about it. or  Draw a picture. or 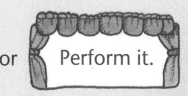 Perform it.

Play a line, draw a

You can play or sing a line of music.

MEET
Wynton Marsalis

Wynton Marsalis is a trumpet player. He plays many kinds of music.

 LISTEN as he tells you about playing the trumpet.

Wynton Marsalis

 Entrada

LISTENING

 from *The Indian Queen*
by *Henry Purcell*

In this piece, the trumpet plays lines of music.

42

line, dance a line

M E E T
Debbie Allen

Debbie Allen is a dancer and choreographer. She plans the steps for dances based on the sound of the music.

Debbie Allen

LISTEN to Debbie Allen talk about planning a dance. Plan a line dance.

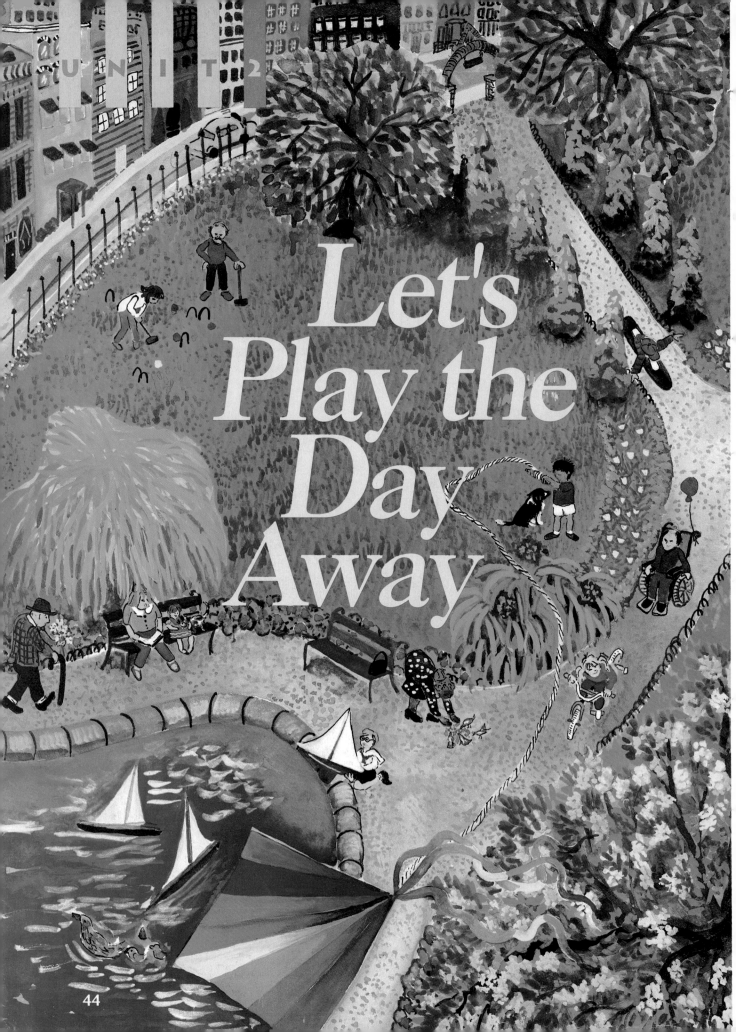

Let's Play the Day Away

Morning Song

Today is a day to catch tadpoles.
Today is a day to explore.
Today is a day to get started.
Come on! Let's not sleep anymore.

Outside the sunbeams are dancing.
The leaves sing a rustling song.
Today is a day for adventures,
and I hope that you'll come along!

—Bobbi Katz

45

GAMES *to* Share

Here is a game from Japan. You can play it with a friend anytime, anywhere!

TAP your fists with the beat as you play the game.

Se, Se, Se

Japanese Hand Game

Japanese:	せ	せ	せ	の	よい	よい	よい
Pronunciation:	se	se	se	no	yoi	yoi	yoi

お	ちゃ	ら	か	お	ちゃ	ら	か	お	ちゃ	ら	か	ほい
o	cha	la	ka	o	cha	la	ka	o	cha	la	ka	hoi

Play the game with a partner.

SHOW rock, paper, or scissors
on the last beat of the song.

rock

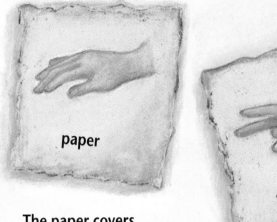

paper

scissors

The rock breaks
the scissors.

The paper covers
the rock.

The scissors cut
the paper.

In Japan, the winners
raise their hands, and
the losers give a bow.

SEE A COLOR, CLAP A SOUND

In "Color Rhythms" below, the blue bars stand for beats. The color blocks stand for sounds. On which beats will you hear sound? No sound?

Think the beat.

CLAP and **SAY** *red* or *yellow.*

MOVE your hands apart for the beat bars without color blocks.

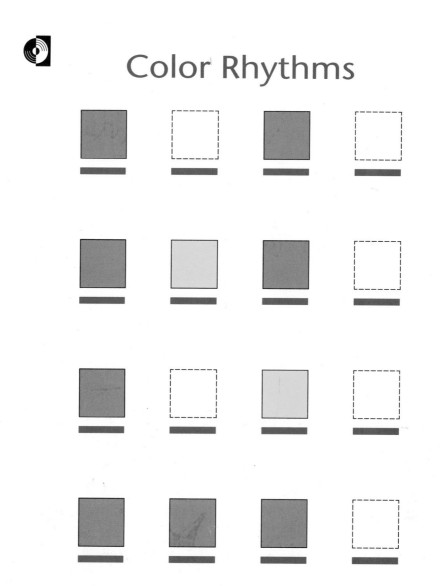

Color Rhythms

Acte III: Symphony

from *The Indian Queen*
by Henry Purcell

This music tells a story about a queen who could not understand her dream.

LISTEN as you clap "Color Rhythms."

THINK IT THROUGH

Compare the picture with the "Color Rhythms" pattern. What is the same? What is different? How might you "play" the picture?

Estate of P. Mondrian/E. M. Holtzman Trust, New York/Giraudon/Art Resource, NY

Composition with Red, Blue, and Yellow, **Piet Mondrian, 1930.**

WHAT CAN A SONG DO?

A song can be used as a greeting. It's like singing hello. This greeting song is from Zimbabwe. You might greet a friend in Zimbabwe by saying *sorida*.

Here are the movements for the song.

so-

ri-

da

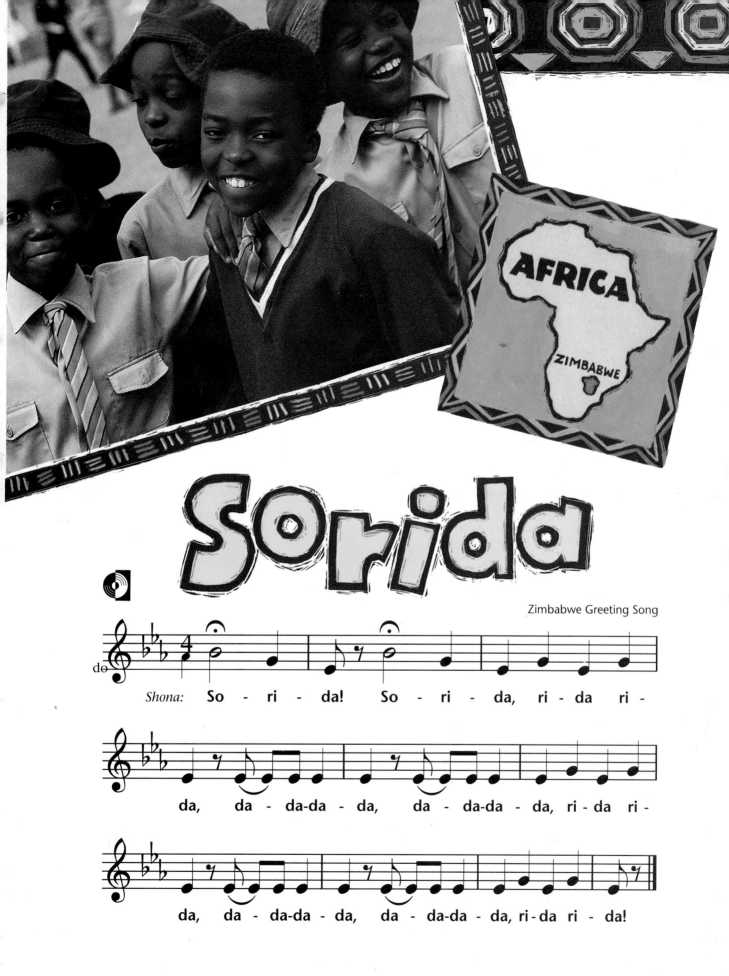

Sorida

Zimbabwe Greeting Song

Shona: So - ri - da! So - ri - da, ri - da ri -
da, da - da-da-da, da - da-da-da, ri - da ri -
da, da - da-da-da, da - da-da-da, ri - da ri - da!

A song can also tell a story.
Who are the people in this story?

Mother Mother

American Jump Rope Game

Mother, Mother, I am sick,
Call for the doctor, quick, quick, quick!

In came the doctor, in came the nurse,
In came the lady with the alligator purse.

I don't want the doctor, I don't want the nurse,
I don't want the lady with the alligator purse.

Out went the doctor, out went the nurse,
Out went the lady with the alligator purse.

Look at the doctor bags.
They show you how high or low
each pitch is in "Mother, Mother."

Moth - er,   Moth - er,   I   am   sick,

Call   for the doc - tor,   Quick,   quick,   quick!

Find the lowest doctor bag.

POINT to the bag for each pitch as you sing.

Let Music

trotting

galloping

One way to enjoy music is to move as you listen.

Look at ways you can move through the space in your room. Try each one.

jumping

walking

Move You

MOVE through your space as you listen to this song. Stop when you hear *Whoa!*

Trot, Old Joe

Texas Folk Song

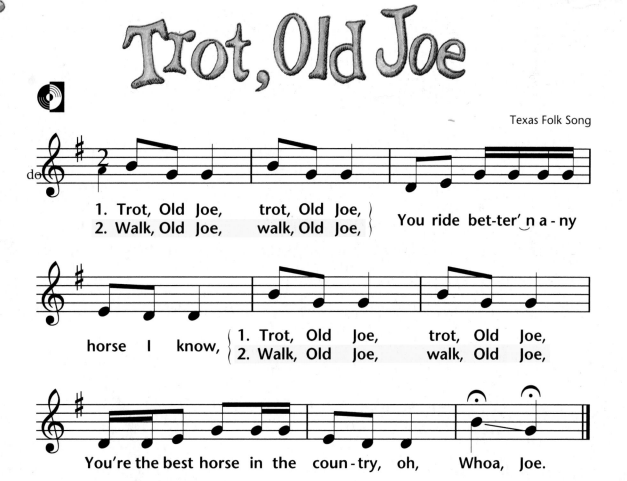

1. Trot, Old Joe,   trot, Old Joe,
2. Walk, Old Joe,   walk, Old Joe,

You ride bet-ter'n a-ny horse I know,

1. Trot, Old Joe,   trot, Old Joe,
2. Walk, Old Joe,   walk, Old Joe,

You're the best horse in the coun-try, oh, Whoa, Joe.

3. Gallop, Old Joe, . . .   4. Jump, Old Joe, . . .

MOVE WHEN THE MUSIC CHANGES

Music can be loud or soft. Think about how you moved to "Trot, Old Joe." Would you move differently if the music were louder? Softer? How would your movements change?

LISTEN to **"Acte III: Symphony."**

Move your hands apart when the music is loud and closer together when it is soft.

loud

soft

MAKE a big shape when the music is loud and a small shape when it is soft.

Sometimes it's fun to sing about how you feel!
Music can be loud or soft. So can grumbling.
A soft grumble can be called a *mumble.*

Do you ever grumble about your chores?
What can you do to make things better?

MUMBLE, GRUMBLE

Words and Music by Minnie O'Leary

Swing
Verse *p*

1. You won - der why I sing ___ the blues.
2. Big Sis - ter tells me, "Clean ___ your room!"

My Dad - dy al - ways makes me tie ___ my shoes!
I'd real - ly like to throw a - way ___ the broom.

My Mom - my, when she combs ___ my hair,
My Grand - ma tells me, "Wash ___ your face!"

Finds tan - gles that are - n't e - ven there!
I wan - na throw the soap to out - er space.

Refrain

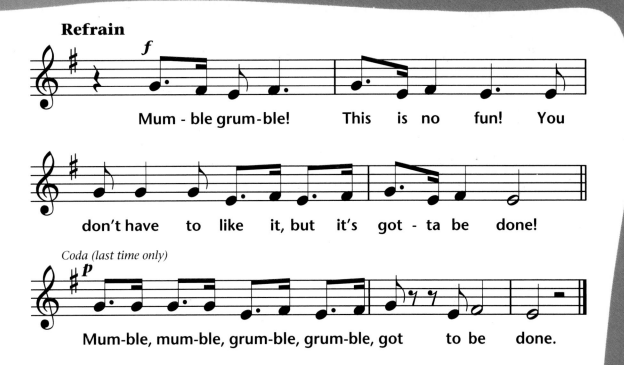

Mum - ble grum-ble! This is no fun! You don't have to like it, but it's got - ta be done!

Coda (last time only)

Mum-ble, mum-ble, grum-ble, grum-ble, got to be done.

3. My Grandpa tells me, "Clean your plate!"
   It's filled with gunky stuff I really hate!
   My Daddy says, "Now go to bed!"
   Just when I'd do most anything instead.

Time for a Rest

When you listen to music, you might think about the sounds you hear. But silences in music are important, too.

A **rest** is the name for silence in music. One sign for a rest is ♩

CLAP and **READ** the rhythm below.

Say *quick* for ♩

Say *sand-wich* for ♫

Be silent for ♩

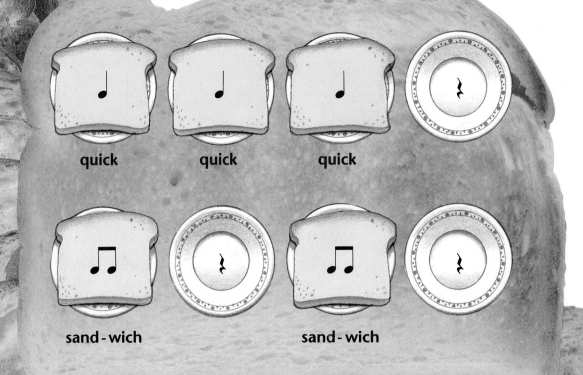

quick   quick   quick

sand-wich   sand-wich

FIND the rests in "Toaster Time."

SAY the words of the poem as you clap the rhythm.

Poem by Eve Merriam

Tick   tick   tick   tick   tick   tick   tick.

Toast   up   a   sand-wich   Quick   quick   quick.

Ham-wich or   jam-wich,   Lick   lick   lick!

Tick   tick   tick   tick   tick   tick - stop!

POP!

Learn a singing game that children in the United States have played for many years.

CLAP each rhythm.

Say *pin* for ♩

Say *pen-ny* for ♫

FIND these rhythms in "Who Has the Penny?"

Who Has the Penny?

American Singing Game

♫ are called **eighth notes.**

They show two sounds to a beat.

♩ is called a **quarter note.**

It shows one sound to a beat.

𝄽 is called a **quarter rest.**

It shows a beat of silence.

do IS LOW

Get ready to learn a new pitch! Once you know it, you'll be able to read the music for many songs.

Point to the higher, middle, and lower bags.

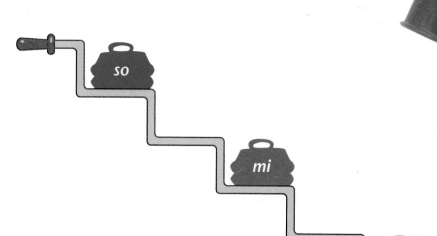

Do is a pitch below *mi*.
How many steps below *mi* is *do*?

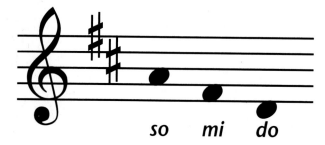

so   mi   do

You can read this song!

FIND *do* in "Mother, Mother."

NAME the pitches and clap the rhythm.

Then sing the song and play the game.

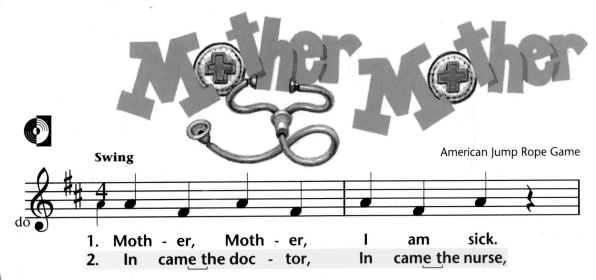

American Jump Rope Game

Swing

1. Moth - er,   Moth - er,   I   am   sick.
2. In   came the doc - tor,   In   came the nurse,

Call   for the doc - tor   Quick, quick, quick!
In   came the la-dy with the   al-li - ga-tor purse.

3. I don't want the doctor,
   I don't want the nurse,
   I don't want the lady
   With the alligator purse.

4. Out went the doctor,
   Out went the nurse,
   Out went the lady
   With the alligator purse.

SO MI DO

So mi and *do* are
names of pitches we
sing and play.

Do is the lowest pitch
of the three.

SHOW *so mi* or *do* **with your body.**
Then sing the whole pattern made by
the class.

Sing two short patterns that you see.
Is there a *so-so-do* pattern along the way?

THINK IT THROUGH

Make a longer pattern by putting two shorter ones together. Decide which patterns you like and why.

Every line and space on the staff is a step. If *do* moves down a step, *mi* and *so* also move down a step.

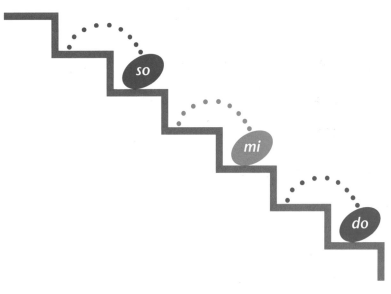

If *do* moves up to a line on the staff, *mi* will move to the line above it.

TELL where *so* will go.

so   mi   do

f and *p*

What Are We?

What is the loudest sound you've ever heard?
In music, the word for loud is **forte.**
The word for soft is **piano.**
The signs for *forte* and *piano* are *f* and *p*.

Listen and watch for the signs *f* and *p* in this camp song. Do you know anyone whose name is this long?

John Jacob Jingleheimer Schmidt

American Camp Song

John Jacob Jingleheimer Schmidt,

His name is my name too.

When-ev-er I go out, The peo-ple al-ways shout,

"There goes John Ja-cob Jing-le-heim-er

Last time only

Schmidt," Da da da da da da da da.

PLAY IT ON THE RADIO

Do you like to listen to the radio softly or loudly? Play a radio game that uses both *forte* and *piano*.

Spotlight on

Paul Hindemith

Paul Hindemith was a German composer who became an American citizen. He wanted to write music that anyone could play and enjoy. One of his pieces even has a part for the audience to sing!

He composed "Puisque tout passe" by choosing a poem, then writing music to go with it. The words are in French. They mean "Quick! Let's sing a song before the day is over."

LISTENING

Puisque tout passe

from *Six Chansons*
by *Paul Hindemith*

LISTEN to how this composer uses *forte* and *piano.*

POINT to the radio that matches each sound.

forte (*f*)

piano (*p*)

SING "John Jacob Jingleheimer Schmidt" again.

Pretend to be the radio music.
Sing louder or softer.

REST YOUR RHYTHM

Sometimes sitting at a window or on a front stoop is called "stoopin'."

MIDSUMMER NIGHT IN HARLEM

Palmer C. Hayden wanted to share his African American culture with others. He painted this picture to show people enjoying a summer evening in Harlem.

Stoopin' on the Window

Swing
f

African American Singing Game

Stoop-in' on the win - dow, wind the ball! ___

(second time)

Stoop-in' on the win - dow, wind the ball! ___ Let's

p   **f**

wind the ball, ___ a - gain, a - gain, a - gain. Let's

p   **f**

wind the ball, ___ a - gain, a - gain, a - gain. Un -

p   **f**

wind the ball, ___ a - gain, a - gain, a - gain. Un -

p

wind the ball, ___ a - gain, a - gain, a - gain.

MAKING RHYTHMS TOGETHER

This rhythm game is for two groups. Group 1 claps Rhythm 1. Group 2 claps Rhythm 2.

CLAP your group's pattern as the other group claps theirs.

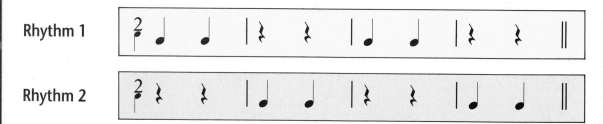

THINK IT THROUGH

Close your eyes and listen to the rhythms. Can you tell where the rests are? Why or why not?

LISTENING

Kecak

Kecak music from Bali is made by several groups of people.

The men say different rhythm patterns using chuk. Each pattern has rests at different times.

All the patterns fit together to make one piece of music.

One man makes a sound as a signal. It tells the other men to get soft or loud.

The music goes with a play. Sometimes the men pretend to be monkeys. They make monkey sounds by saying chuk over and over.

LISTEN to "Kecak." Do you hear the different rhythm patterns?

Make Music with Your Speaking Voice

This poem has words that could be loud or soft. Can you find them as you read?

At the TOP of My VOICE

When I stamp
The ground thunders,
When I shout
The world rings,
When I sing
The air wonders
How I do such things.

—Felice Holman

CHOOSE where you will make your voice loud or soft.

SIZZLE A SONG

You can "sizzle" a song. Use your tongue to make a *ts* sound.

You can sizzle in lots of ways!
>   You can echo rhythms that you hear.
>   You can make up sizzle rhythms for others to echo.
>   You can sizzle the rhythm of a song.
> Try some out!

THE CHORUS TELLS A TALE

There are many ways besides singing to make music with your voice.

The "Cak" chorus helps to tell a story. Sometimes they pretend to be monkeys or trees. Sometimes they save the actors from danger.

Can you tell when the music will be loud?

LISTENING MAP *Listen to "Kecak." Notice how the musicians use their voices. Point to the f or p that matches what you hear.*

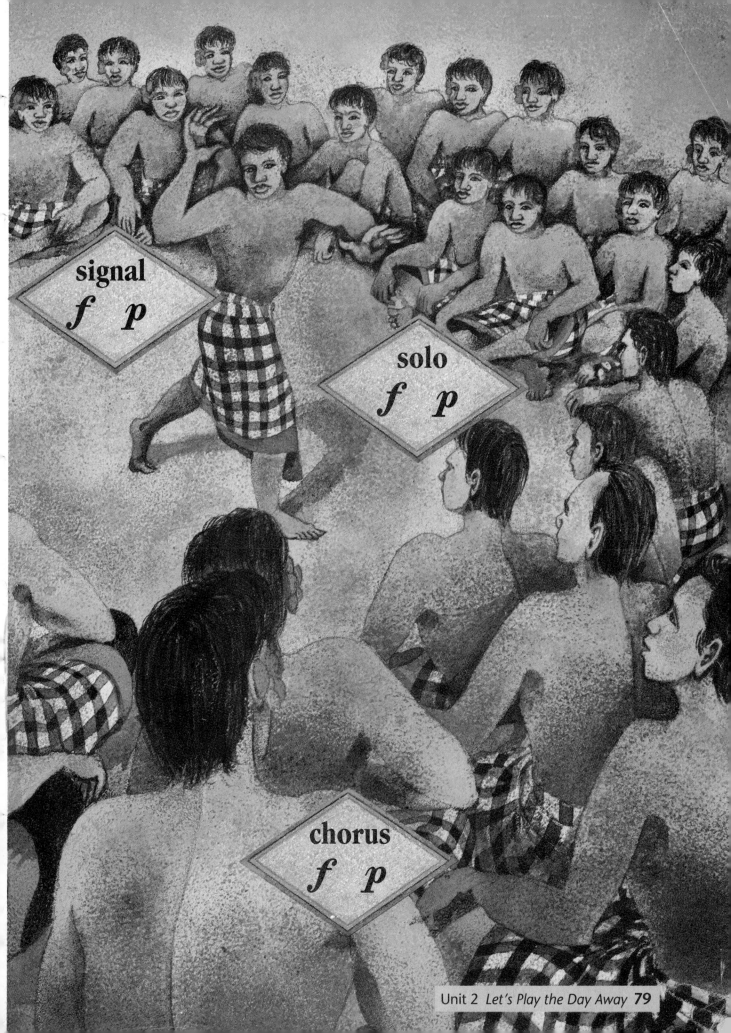

signal **f** **p**

solo **f** **p**

chorus **f** **p**

REVIEW

WELCOME TO GAMELAND!

Follow this game path.
Stop and play each game.

START

80

Which songs use *so mi* and *do*?

Which songs or poems use rests?

CHECK IT OUT

1. On which beat bar do you hear a rest?

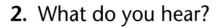

---

2. What do you hear?

a.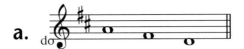

b.

c.

---

3. Choose the rhythm you hear.

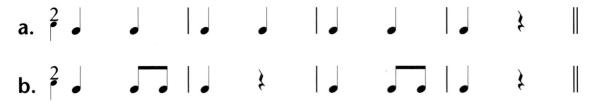

---

4. Which melody do you hear?

a.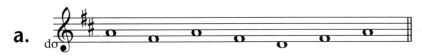

b.

c.

 # CREATE

MAKE UP your own melody using *so mi do*.

Clap this rhythm.

Plan one pitch for each note head.
Don't plan pitches for the rests. They
have no sound.
Write your plan on a piece of paper.

**PLAY your song on an instrument.
Use C for *so*. Use A for *mi*. Use F for *do*.**

Share

Choose a game you like. Teach a friend
how to play.

Write the directions.   or   Write about how you
taught the game.

Encore

The Nutcracker

In a **ballet,** the dance and the music tell a story. The story of the ballet *The Nutcracker* is about a little girl named Clara. She receives a nutcracker as a gift at a Christmas party. Clara is very happy with the funny-looking nutcracker. Her happiness is spoiled when her brother steals and then breaks the gift.

March

Overture

LISTENING The Nutcracker

by *Piotr Ilyich Tchaikovsky*

Listen to the story and music of this famous ballet. Learn more about Clara and the Nutcracker.

LOOK at the pictures to find out about the dances and characters in the story.

How does the music change for each dance? Which dance would you like to do?

PLAN your own dance for each piece.

Waltz of the Flowers

Dance of the Sugar Plum Fairy

Chinese Dance

Take a
New Path

Until I Saw the Sea

Until I saw the sea
I did not know
that wind
could wrinkle water so.

I never knew
that sun
could splinter a whole sea of blue.

Nor
did I know before,
a sea breathes in and out
upon a shore.

—Lilian Moore

INSTRUMENT FAMILIES

Have you ever heard someone talking and known who it was by the sound of his or her voice? Just as each person's voice is different and special, so are the "voices" of instruments.

Instruments that sound exact pitches are called **pitched instruments.**

Some instruments do not sound exact pitches. They are called **unpitched instruments.**

There are four families of unpitched instruments. Each unpitched instrument belongs in at least one of the families. A few can belong to more than one family!

LISTEN to the sounds of each instrument family. Point to the family you hear.

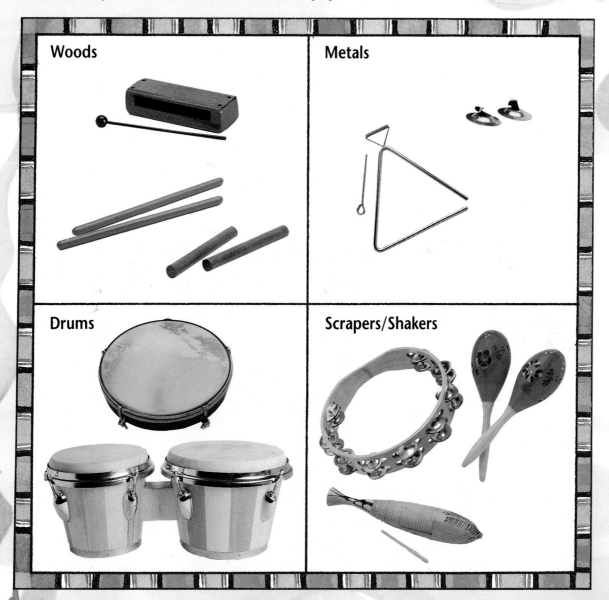

Woods

Metals

Drums

Scrapers/Shakers

THINK IT THROUGH

Compare the four families of unpitched instruments. What makes each one different? Are there some things that are the same?

SOUNDS AT SEA

At sea, you can hear many sounds. Some may remind you of the sound of a particular instrument.

Here's a silly song about a sailor. As you sing it, think about how these words sound:

sea

chop

knee

SHOO-BOP

SHUH-BOP

CHOOSE an instrument family to play on
sea, chop, knee, shoo-bop, shuh-bop.

A Sailor Went to Sea, Sea, Sea

American Playground Song

1.–3. A sail - or went to { sea, sea, sea,
chop, chop, chop,
knee, knee, knee,

To see what he could { see, see, see,
chop, chop, chop,
knee, knee, knee,

And all that he could { see, see, see,
chop, chop, chop,
knee, knee, knee,

Was the bot-tom of the deep blue { sea, sea, sea.
chop, chop, chop.
knee, knee, knee.

4. A sailor went to shoo-bop, shuh-bop,
To see what he could shoo-bop, shuh-bop,
And all that he could shoo-bop, shuh-bop,
Was the bottom of the deep blue shoo-bop, shuh-bop.

Getting from Here to There

When you walk from your chair to the door, you take a certain path. Your path makes a line called a **floor pathway.** It can be curved or straight.

TRACE these pathways with your finger.

WALK them on the floor.

Now walk the first letter of your name. Does your letter have any curved pathways?

JAZZ WALK

You can make your walk jazzy. Here's how!

MOVE your feet in a step-touch pattern.
First do your jazz walk in place.
Then do it along a floor pathway.

Kidd Jordan's Second Line

by Dirty Dozen Brass Band

The Dirty Dozen Brass Band plays parade music in a jazzy style. "Kidd Jordan's Second Line" is about people who don't want the parade to end. They get up and follow the band. The "second line" keeps the parade going. It's fun!

JAZZ WALK to "Kidd Jordan's Second Line."
How many beats is each step-touch movement?

FOLLOW THAT CURVE!

What kind of pathway does the ribbon make?

PLAY the game for "Here Comes a Bluebird." Use a curved floor pathway as you go through the "windows."

Here Comes a Bluebird

American Singing Game

Here	comes	a	blue	-	bird,

In	through my	win	-	dow,

Hey,		did	-dle	um	-a

Day,	day,	day.

PLAY sounds that last
two beats with "Here
Comes a Bluebird."

Hey,

Think about the sound of birds singing outside your window. Could you tell by listening if they were flying closer or flying away? How?

This song is about a dove who flies away, never to return home.

"Child with Dove" by Picasso, The National Gallery, London

CHILD WITH DOVE
Pablo Picasso was a very famous painter. He enjoyed painting children of all ages.

FIND the *p* and *f*.

What do they tell you about singing the song?

La paloma se fue
The Dove That Flew Away

Puerto Rican Folk Song
Arranged by Alejandro Jiménez
English Version by MMH

Gently *p*

Spanish: ¿Se - ño - res no han vis - to la pa -
English: Has an - y - one seen him? The ___

lo - ma que vo - ló del pa - lo - mar?
dove that flew a - way and left his home.

f

Se fue la pa - lo - ma, se fue la pa - lo - ma, se
He's gone, *la pa - lo - ma,* he's gone, *la pa - lo - ma,* he's

fue pa - ra no vol - ver.
gone, nev - er to re - turn.

At carnival time in Cuba, there are large parades. Everyone dances, and bands play. The sound of a parade gets louder as it comes closer. What happens to the sound as the parade moves away?

This sign means get louder.

crescendo

This sign means get softer.

decrescendo

LISTENING

La comparsa *by Ernesto Lecuona*

LISTENING MAP *Trace the outline of the map as you hear a* **crescendo** *and* **decrescendo**.

crescendo

SPOTLIGHT ON
ERNESTO LECUONA

When Ernesto Lecuona was a boy in Cuba, he liked music very much. He studied piano at a special music school. He wrote his first song when he was only eleven years old! Mr. Lecuona wrote this piano music to show how a parade might sound as it goes by.

decrescendo

A Note to Notice

There are some kinds of music that make you want to move!

DO your jazz walk to "Kidd Jordan's Second Line."

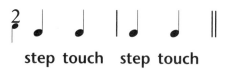

step touch   step touch

Now skate from one step to the next. You can show the rhythm of your walk like this:

skate   skate

Two quarter notes tied together show a sound that lasts two beats. The **tie sign** looks like this:

A HALF NOTE

Here is another way to show
a sound that lasts two beats.
It is called a **half note**.

So... ♩ ♩ = 𝅗𝅥

DO this fancy walk as you say *step touch*
for quarter notes and *skate* for half notes.

step touch   step touch   skate   skate

HUNT THE HALF NOTE

Here's a rhythm that uses notes and rests you know.

FIND the half notes (♩).

Here comes a blue - bird in through my win - dow,

Hey, did - dle - um - a day, day, day.

CLAP the rhythm of "Here Comes a Bluebird."

Use a clap-circle motion for the half notes. Clap once, then make a circle in the air with your hands together.

Say *bird* for ♩

flying for ♫

hey for ♩

Sing this song using what you know about half notes. When you sing *hey,* and sometimes *day,* you sing them for two beats.

American Singing Game

Here Comes a Bluebird

do

Here comes a blue - bird in through my win - dow,

Hey, did - dle - um - a day, day, day.

Takes him-self a part - ner, hops in the gar - den,

Hey, did - dle - um - a day, day, day.

Under and Over the Sea

Sea creatures make pathways as they swim under the water.

Toward the City

by Edward Christmas

Swim your own pathways as you listen to "Toward the City." What does this music make you think of?

EDWARD

CHRISTMAS

Edward Christmas wrote and performed "Toward the City." When Mr. Christmas was nine years old, he began playing the flute. His favorite type of flute is the bass flute—he enjoys its rich, deep tone.

MOVE and match your pathway to the instrument you hear.

PADDLE A PATHWAY

In Nigeria, some people fish in long boats.
Everyone in the boat must paddle together.
When they see storm clouds, they must paddle
faster to get home.

SING this paddling song
slowly. Then sing it faster.

PADDLE together to
keep your boat going.

EH SOOM BOO KAWAYA

NIGERIAN BOAT SONG

Nigerian Song

Vocables: Eh soom boo ka - wa - ya ke - dou, ka - dee.

Eh soom boo ka - wa - ya ke - dou, ka - dee.

To what family does each African instrument belong?

slit drum

talking drum

double bell

rattle

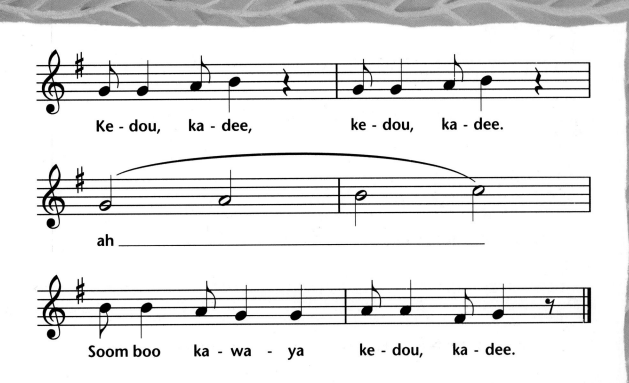

Ke - dou, ka - dee, ke - dou, ka - dee.

ah _____

Soom boo ka - wa - ya ke - dou, ka - dee.

Plan instrument parts to play with
"Eh Soom Boo Kawaya."

CHOOSE an unpitched
instrument to play each line.

PLAY the half notes through
the whole song.

Eh | soom boo ka - wa - ya |

| ke - dou, ka - dee. ||

TWO-BEAT SOUNDS

AROUND THE WORLD

In Alaska, people wear flat boots to walk on snow. They walk carefully and slowly. Pretend to walk on deep snow. Put each foot down gently. Look behind you! Your footprints have made a pathway in the snow!

Mount McKinley in Alaska is the tallest mountain in North America.

Native Americans called Athabascans sing this song about Mount McKinley. Their name for the mountain is *Denali.* It means *the great one* or *the high one.*

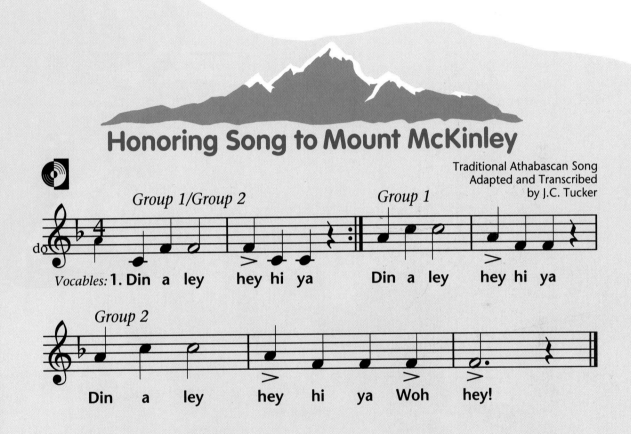

Honoring Song to Mount McKinley

Traditional Athabascan Song
Adapted and Transcribed
by J.C. Tucker

Group 1/Group 2

Group 1

Vocables: **1. Din a ley   hey hi ya   Din a ley   hey hi ya**

Group 2

Din   a   ley   hey   hi   ya   Woh   hey!

2. Whu pa hey hey hi ya
Whu pa hey hey hi ya
Whu pa hey hey hi ya Woh hey!

WALK to half notes as you listen to the song.

READ the rhythms in the song.

Clap for ♩

Slide your hands on your knees for ♩

LET'S FLY TO PUERTO RICO

"Honoring Song to Mount McKinley" has several half notes. Listen for half notes in "La paloma se fue."

The children want the dove to come back.
They say:

Dove, dove,   dove, dove,   Dove, dove,   come back, lit - tle dove.

Help the children call the dove.
Remember that each half note lasts two beats.

SAIL ON TO ENGLAND

FIND the half notes in this rhyme from England.

READ the rhythm.

Clap for ♩

Slide your hands on your legs for ♩

Choose a movement for ♫ and 𝄽

DONKEY, DONKEY

Old English Rhyme

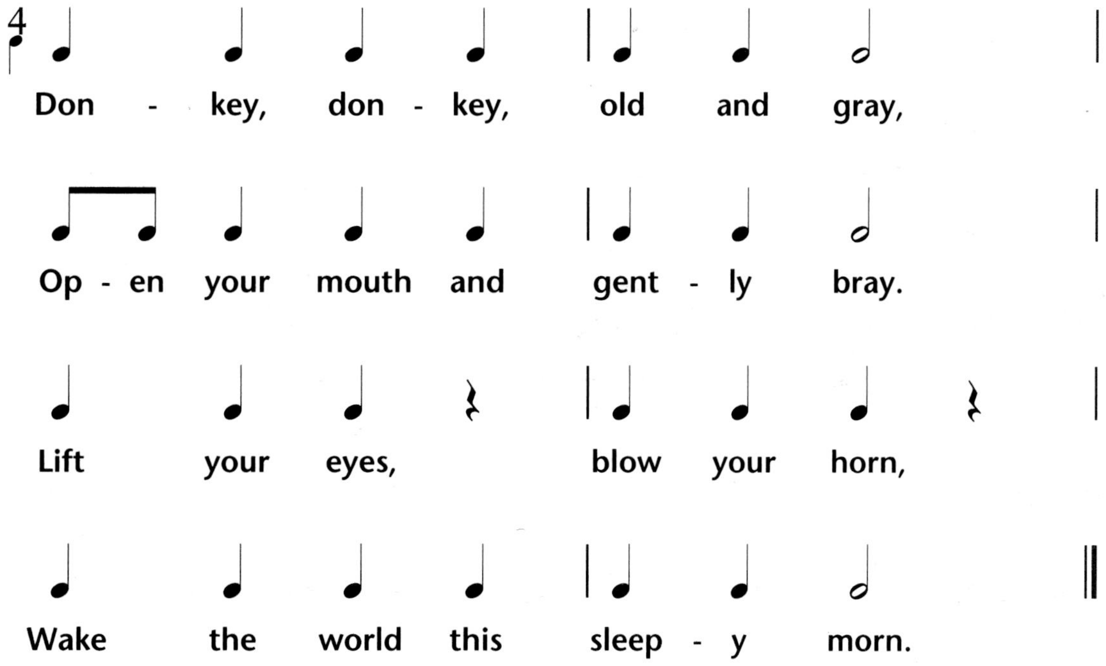

Don - key, don - key, old and gray,

Op - en your mouth and gent - ly bray.

Lift your eyes, blow your horn,

Wake the world this sleep - y morn.

MAKE A MELODY

You know the pitches *do mi so* and *la*.
One pitch after another makes
a **melody.** Melodies can move up,
down, or stay the same.

la

so

mi

do

ECHO-SING or ECHO-PLAY the melodies you hear.

Do the melodies go up, down, or stay the same?

Here's one way you can make up your own melody! Start with a rhythm you can play or sing many times. You can use the rhythm below.

This sign :‖ tells you to go back to the beginning and repeat. Find the repeat sign.

Hee   haw!   Lis-ten to his horn!

READ and **CLAP** the rhythm.

Now add some pitches.
You know *do mi so* and *la.*

Sing or play the rhythm on each pitch.
Try the rhythm using two pitches.
Listen carefully.
Choose which two pitches to use.
Decide when to play each pitch.

THINK IT THROUGH

Do you like the melody you made?
Name one thing you might do in a
different way the next time.

**SING or play your melody
for a friend.**

One Hand, Then the Other

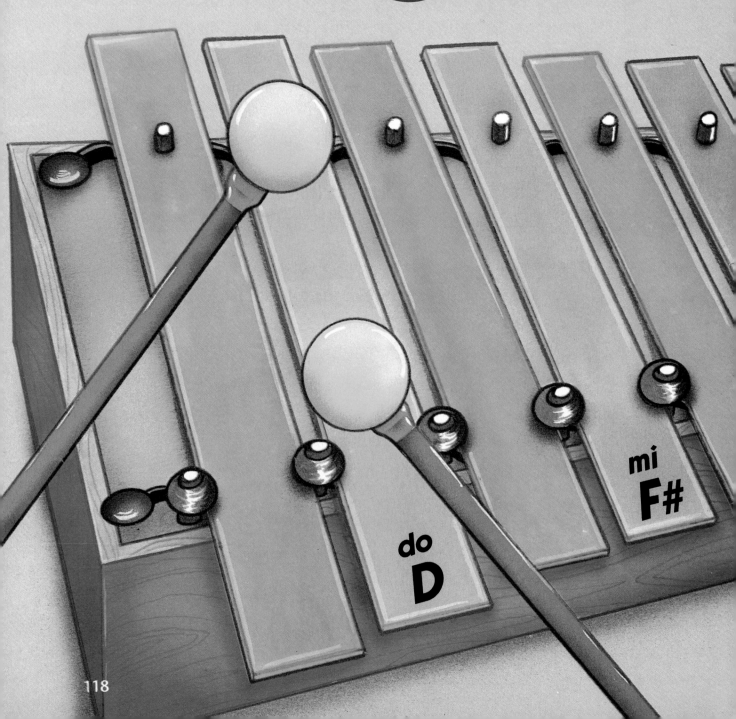

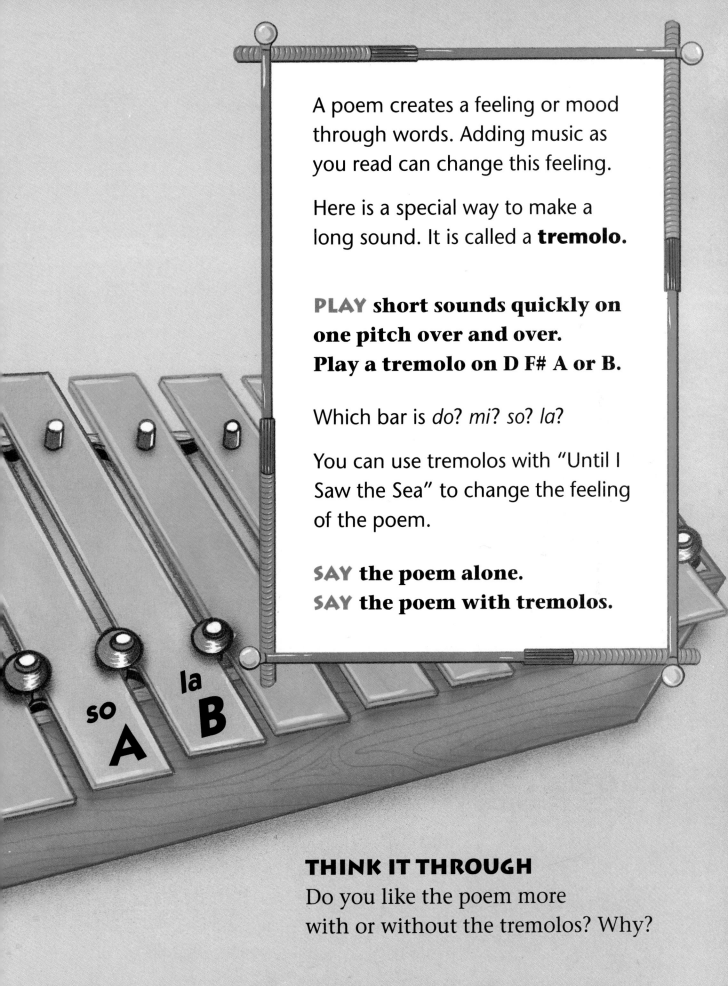

A poem creates a feeling or mood through words. Adding music as you read can change this feeling.

Here is a special way to make a long sound. It is called a **tremolo.**

PLAY short sounds quickly on one pitch over and over. Play a tremolo on D F# A or B.

Which bar is *do? mi? so? la?*

You can use tremolos with "Until I Saw the Sea" to change the feeling of the poem.

SAY the poem alone.
SAY the poem with tremolos.

THINK IT THROUGH
Do you like the poem more with or without the tremolos? Why?

DONKEY, DONKEY

Old English Rhyme
Music by Margaret Campbelle-duGard

Don-key, don-key, old and gray, O-pen your mouth and gent-ly bray.

Lift your eyes, blow your horn, Wake the world this sleep-y morn.

READ the poem below.

Use your voice to tell the story.
Add instruments on the rhyming words.

If I Had a Donkey

If I had a donkey that wouldn't go,
Would I beat him? Oh, no, no.
I'd put him in the barn and give him some corn,
The best little donkey that ever was born.

—Jacob Beuler

SING this ending.

Wake the world this sleep - y morn. __

TRAVELING TREASURES

Kidd Jordan has found a
treasure map! Jazz-walk to
his house and help him
follow the map!

The map says to find a
sailor and go to sea.

Take time for a swim.
There are treasures
under the sea.

You're in Nigeria! Take a
boat ride on the river.
When you see rain clouds,
paddle back to land.

You have found treasures
all along the way. Which
ones surprised you?

 HECK IT OUT

1. Which instrument family do you hear?

a. drums   **b.** metals   **c.** woods   **d.** scrapers/shakers

---

2. Choose the rhythm you hear.

a.

b.

c.

---

3. Which rhythm do you hear?

a.

b.

c.

---

4. Which order do you hear?

a. woods   metals   drums   scrapers/shakers

b. metals   woods   drums   scrapers/shakers

c. scrapers/shakers   drums   metals   woods

CREATE

CHOOSE sounds to help tell the story of **Romper, Stomper, and Boo.**

Choose one rhythm for each elephant. Then choose an instrument family to play each rhythm.

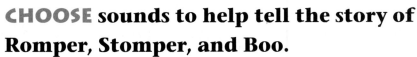

a.

b.

c.

TELL the story. Add your rhythms for each elephant.

Share

Write your own story. Where will it take place? Who are the characters?

Make up sounds for your characters.

Write your story.   or   Tell your story.

EXPLORE A

The electronic keyboard can make
and change sounds in many ways.
Some of the buttons on the keyboard
can be pressed to make louder
and softer sounds.

louder   softer

lower

Look at the
picture of the electronic
keyboard to see the ways in which
sounds can be made and changed.

PLAY a keyboard to hear the different

KEYBOARD

EXPLORE the ways in which sounds are made. How can these sounds be changed?

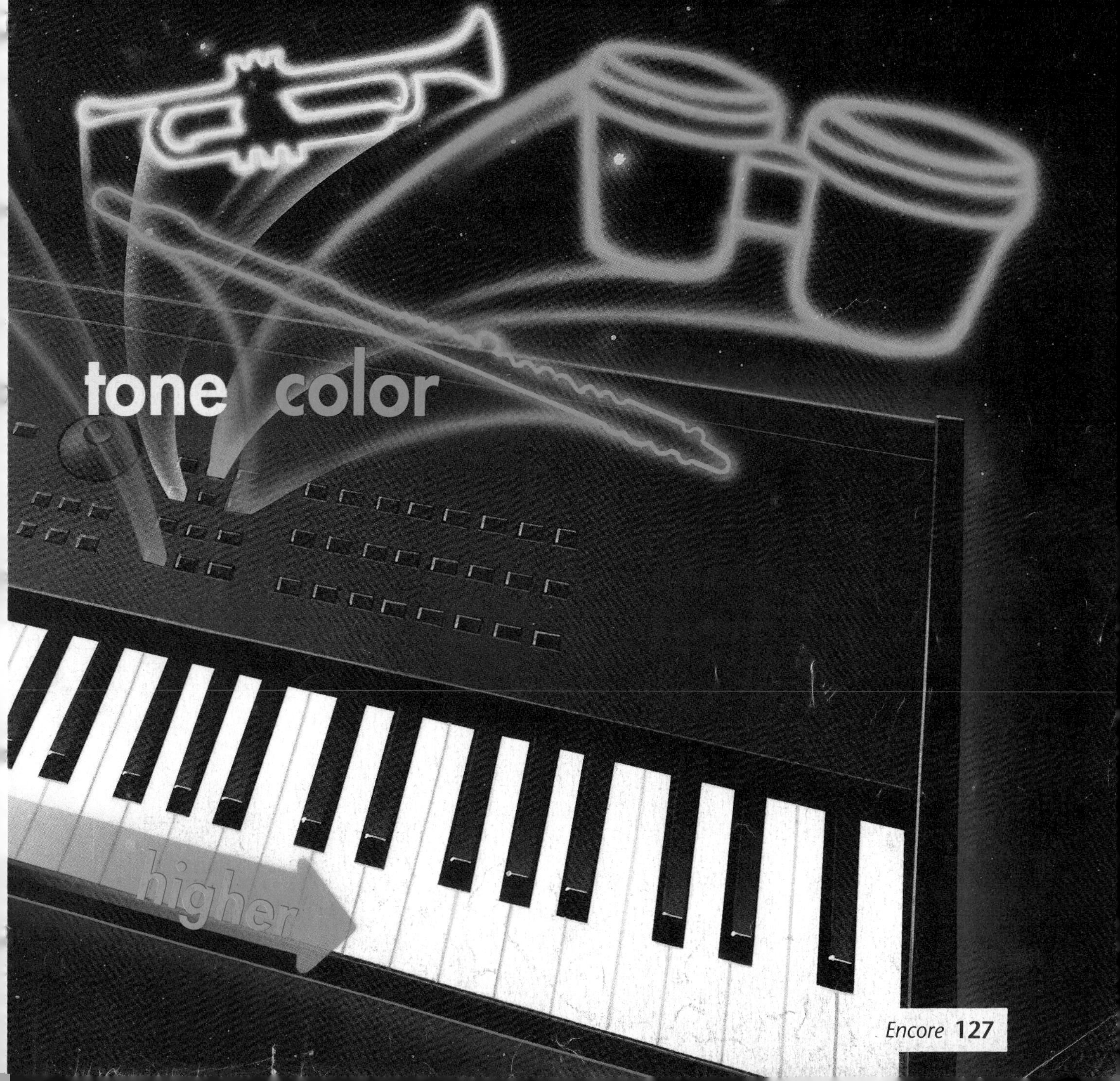

tone color

higher

UNIT 4

THE SKY'S THE LIMIT

SKYSCRAPER

Skyscraper, skyscraper
Scrape me some sky.
Tickle the sun
While the stars go by.

Tickle the stars
While the sun's climbing high,
Then skyscraper, skyscraper
Scrape me some sky.

—*Dennis Lee*

Baseball has been a favorite game in the United States for more than 100 years. This song has been around for almost that long! People still enjoy singing it when they go to baseball games.

Take Me Out to the Ball Game

Music by Albert von Tilzer
Words by Jack Norworth

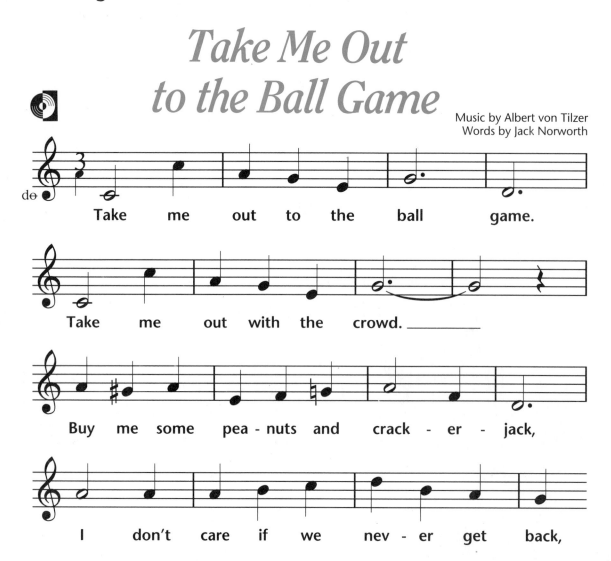

Take me out to the ball game.

Take me out with the crowd. _____

Buy me some pea - nuts and crack - er - jack,

I don't care if we nev - er get back,

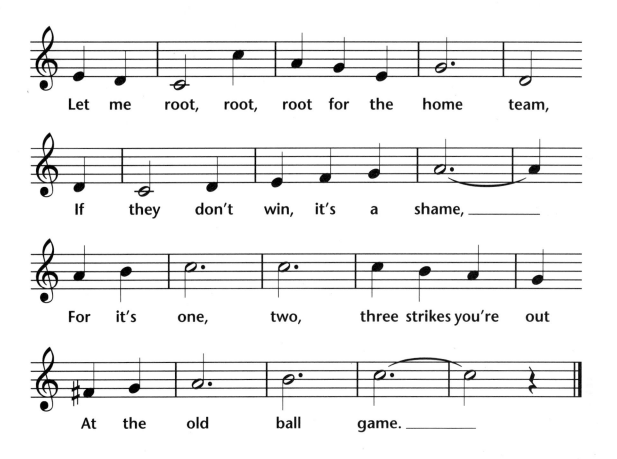

Let me root, root, root for the home team,

If they don't win, it's a shame, _____

For it's one, two, three strikes you're out

At the old ball game. _____

When you go to a baseball game, you might cheer for your team by saying "We want a hit!" over and over.

An **ostinato** is a musical pattern that repeats over and over.

SAY this ostinato as you listen to "Take Me Out to the Ball Game."

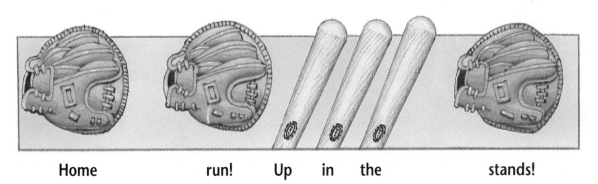

Home   run!   Up   in   the   stands!

Fireworks often add to the fun of outdoor events.

LISTENING **Minuet** from *Royal Fireworks Music* by **George Frideric Handel**

 Listen to **Royal Fireworks Music.** *The first time it was performed, there were so many fireworks that the bandshell caught on fire!*

When George Frideric Handel was eight, he taught himself to play the harpsichord. Late at night, he would practice very softly so no one could hear. Handel became one of England's most famous composers.

The minuet was a popular dance during the time that Handel lived. Minuet music moves in sets of three. Try these steps for a minuet.

Step in, step out

Trade places

Walk forward

CREATE your own movements for a minuet.

LISTENING MAP *Follow the map as you listen to "Minuet." Each box goes with a different part of the music.*

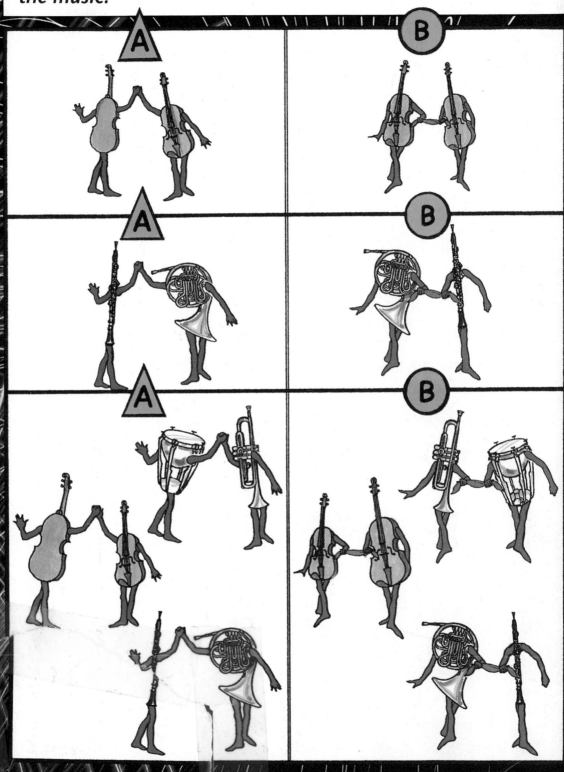

MOVE to "Minuet." Use a different movement for each part of the music.

LOOKING FOR A NEW

Pitch

Sally's always looking for something new.
Today she's looking for a new pitch.
See if you can help her find it!

TRACE a pathway with your finger as you sing.

Sally Go Round the Sun

Nursery Rhyme

Sally go round the sun,
Sally go round the moon,
Sally go round the chimney tops
Every afternoon.
Boom!

"Hop, Old Squirrel" is from Virginia. It is a very old song that people still like to sing. The game is fun, too!

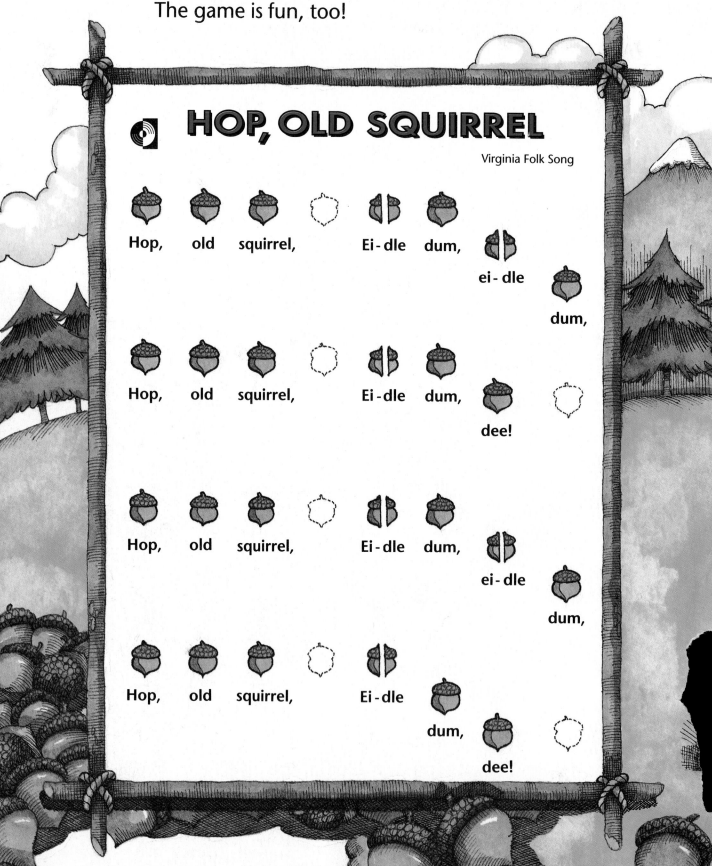

HOP, OLD SQUIRREL

Virginia Folk Song

Hop, old squirrel, Ei-dle dum, ei-dle dum,

Hop, old squirrel, Ei-dle dum, dee!

Hop, old squirrel, Ei-dle dum, ei-dle dum,

Hop, old squirrel, Ei-dle dum, dee!

THE PUZZLE IS SOLVED

SING *trot, Old Joe,*
following the acorns.

SING *eidledum dee,*
following the acorns.

Which pitches in the two songs are the same? Which pitches are different? Where is the new pitch?

Part + Part = WHOLE

Do you have a jigsaw puzzle or a toy that comes apart? Each piece is a part. When you put the parts back together, they make a complete object.

Songs or poems can also have parts, or sections. Sometimes you can even put several together to create something new! Here's how.

SAY "Skyscraper" as you move.

READ "Make a Circle." Then do what the poem tells you to do.

Make a Circle

Make a cir - cle, big and round,

Make it now with - out a sound.

CREATE something new. Try saying one poem right after you say the other. How many sections will there be?

Little Bear had to sleep outside his den. At night, he was too cold. During the day, he was too hot. Why does Little Bear have to stay outside?

MEET ERNEST SIVA

LISTENING

Listen as Ernest Siva tells about learning this song. It has two parts. See if you can tell the first part from the second.

A

Ucha Tirvarch
Little Bear Song

Serrano (Maringa') Indian Lullaby
As Sung by Ernest Siva

1. Ucha ucha tirvarch,
   Ucha ucha tirvarch,
   Kai kwun haipant
   Haipant nukuman.

2. Ucha ucha shruvut,
   Ucha ucha shruvut,
   Kai kwun haipant
   Haipant nukuman.

3. Ircher ircher tamyit
   Ircher ircher tamyit
   Kai kwun haipant
   Haipant nukuman.

FIND pictures for each part of the song.
Point to them as you sing.

The first part is the A section.
The second part is the B section.

The **form** tells the order of the
sections. The form of "Little Bear Song"
is A B A B A B.

B

Refrain
Aya kaich, aya kaich,
Aya kaich, aya kaich,
Aaya, aya kaino, aaya, aya kaino,
Aaya, aya kaino.

Ready for *re*

You know most of the pitches in this song.

FIND *do*. **Sing the pitch syllables.**

FIND the pitch you don't know.

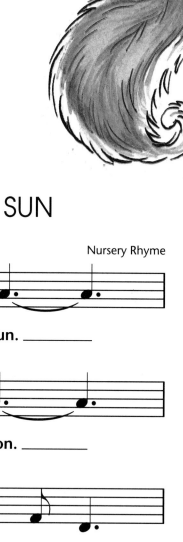

SALLY GO ROUND THE SUN

Nursery Rhyme

Sal - ly go round the sun. _____

Sal - ly go round the moon. _____

Sal - ly go round the chim - ney tops

Ev' - ry af - ter - noon. Boom!

The pitch between *mi* and *do* is **re.**

Which set of tinted notes below matches the acorn pattern?

HOP OLD SQUIRREL

Virginia Folk Song

Hop, old squirrel, Ei - dle dum, ei - dle dum,

Hop, old squirrel, Ei - dle dum, dee!

Hop, old squirrel, Ei - dle dum, ei - dle dum,

Hop, old squirrel, Ei - dle dum, dee!

Can you find *re* in this song?

BUTTON, YOU MUST WANDER

American Singing Game

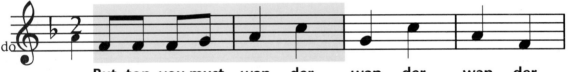

But - ton, you must wan - der, wan - der, wan - der,

But - ton, you must wan - der ev' - ry - where.

Bright eyes will find you, sharp eyes will find you.

But - ton, you must wan - der ev' - ry - where.

The buttons show you where the pitches will be in this song.

SING the first six pitches of "Button, You Must Wander" with pitch syllables. Then sing the whole song with words.

This button is for you!

ASK ME ABOUT *re!*

PLAY this game with a partner.
Do one movement on each beat.
This makes a three-beat pattern.

When you get to *one, two, three strikes you're out,* do one movement every three beats.

THINK IT THROUGH

Are the words *one, two, three* in the song each one beat long? How can you tell?

A DOTTED HALF NOTE

You've learned that a half note is a way to show two beats with one note. Now find out how to show three beats with one note!

READ this ostinato.

Which part of the picture shows a sound that lasts three beats? Which part shows a sound on every beat?

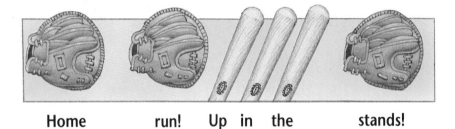

Home   run!   Up   in   the   stands!

FIND the new note below.

You know that a quarter note ♩ shows a sound that is one beat long. A **dotted half note** 𝅗𝅥. shows a sound that is three beats long. It lasts as long as three quarter notes.

READ this rhythm, then play it with "Minuet." Use different instruments for the A section and the B section.

You will play the whole rhythm three times.

Hear It, Say It Sing It, Play It

Learn a game from the Philippines. It will give you a chance to "show off" a little. In Part A, everyone moves. In Part B, one person moves.

TRY out some interesting pathways when it is your turn to move.

HOW DO YOU LEARN A SONG?

You can learn songs in many different ways. Learn "Sasara Ang Bulaklak" this way. It goes with the game you just played.

Listen to the song.
Read the pitches of the first part.
Practice saying the words.
Sing the whole song and play the game.

Sasara Ang Bulaklak

The Flower Fades

Filipino Folk Song
English Version by MMH

A

Tagalog: Sa - sa - ra ang bu - lak - lak,   bu - bu - ka   ang bu - lak - lak,
English: In the fall the flow-er fades,   In the spring the flow-er blooms,

I - i - kot ang bu - lak - lak,   Da - da - an ang rey - na.
Now the flow-er turns a-round,   Make way for the Queen now.

B

Bum ti-ya ya, bum ti-ya ya,   bum ti-ya ya ye - ye
Bum ti-ya ya, bum ti-ya ya,   bum ti ya ya ye - ye

Bum ti-ya ya, bum ti-ya ya, bum ti-ya ya ye - ye a bom!
Bum ti-ya ya, bum ti-ya ya, bum ti-ya ya ye - ye a bom!

LEARN A TRUMPET MELODY

SING the melody in Part B. Then listen as it is played.

LISTENING

Intrade

from *Paralipomena*

by Gunild Keetman

LISTENING MAP   *Follow the map for "Intrade." Can you recognize the trumpet melody when you hear it?*

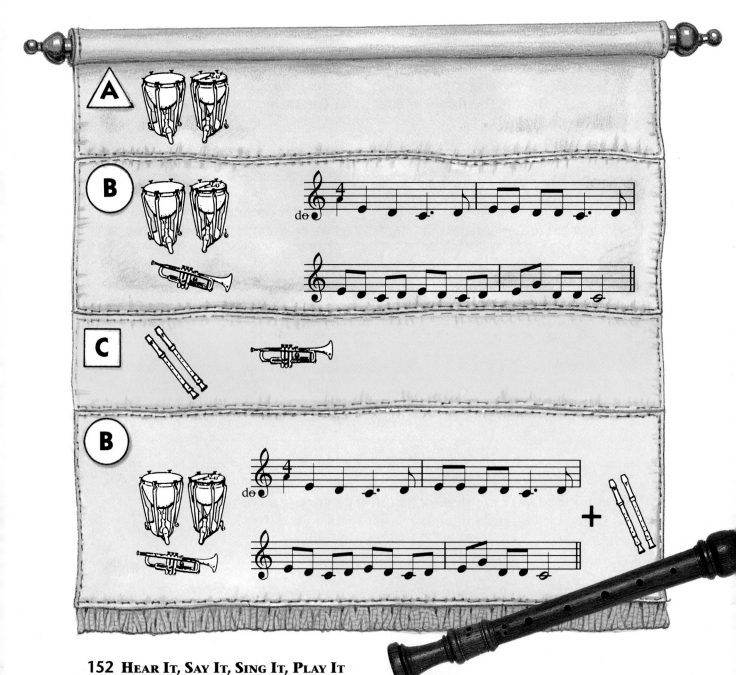

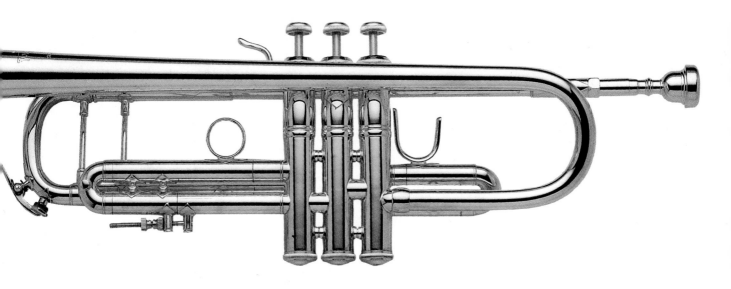

MAKE A MELODY

You know these pitches!

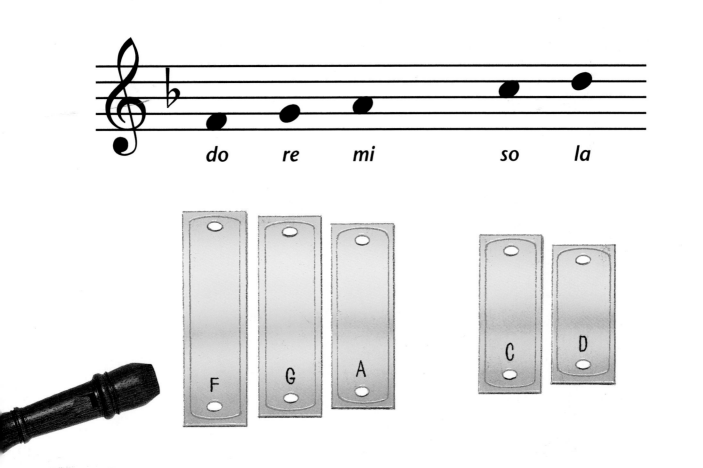

do   *re*   *mi*   *so*   *la*

CREATE your own melody with the pitches you know.

A, B, and Away We Go!

Many songs and games have
two parts—A and B. Name
the ones you know. The
Israeli folk song, "Simi Yadech,"
also has an A and a B part.

154

Find the A and B sections of "Simi Yadech."

MOVE with a partner during the A and B sections. Find a new partner by the end of the B section.

Simi Yadech
Give Me Your Hand

Israeli Folk Song
English Version by MMH

A

Hebrew: שִׁי - מִי - יָ - דֵךְ - בְּ - יָ - דִי - אֶ -
English: Give me your hand, Give me the o - ther,

נִי - שֶׁ - לָךְ - וַ - אַתְּ - שֶׁ - לִי
I'm your ___ friend and you are ___ mine.

B

הֵי הֵי - גַ - ל - יָה - יָה - פֶּה - פִּ - יָה - בַּת - הַ - רִים - יְ -
Hey, hey, my good friend, Take my hand and dance with me.

הֵי הֵי - גַ - ל - יָה - יָה - פֶּה - פִּ - יָה. - בַּת - הַ - רִים - יְ -
Hey, hey, my good friend, Take my hand and dance with me.

TRAVEL AWAY ON THE A-B-A TRAIN

You know many songs that have A B form. But what if a song has A B A form? Tell how you think a song with A B A form will be different from one that has A B form.

Three train cars show different sections of "Git on Board."

POINT to the letters that match each section.

TELL a partner the name of the form.

Da Capo al Fine means to go back to the start, and keep going until you see the word ***Fine.***

Git on Board

African American Spiritual
As Sung by Margaret Campbelle-duGard

A Refrain

Git on board, lit-tle chil-dren, Git on board, lit-tle chil-dren,

End (Fine)

Git on board, lit-tle chil-dren,—There's room for man-y a more.

B Verse

1. The gos-pel train's a - com-in', I hear it close at
2. I hear the bell and whis-tle, The com-ing 'round the

hand, ___ I hear the whis-tle blow - in' and
curve; ___ She's play - ing all her steam and pow'r and

Go back to the beginning and sing to the End.
(Da Capo al Fine)

rum - blin' through the land.
strain - ing ev' - ry nerve.

CIRCLES ALL AROUND

A circle is a kind of pathway that doesn't really have a beginning or an end. You know how to make circles in many different ways.

Each picture shows one way to move in a circle.

SHOW a circle in these different ways. Make a circle by yourself or with others.

Spin and make a circle in the air.

Walk a pathway. Make circles as you go.

Move one body part in a circle.

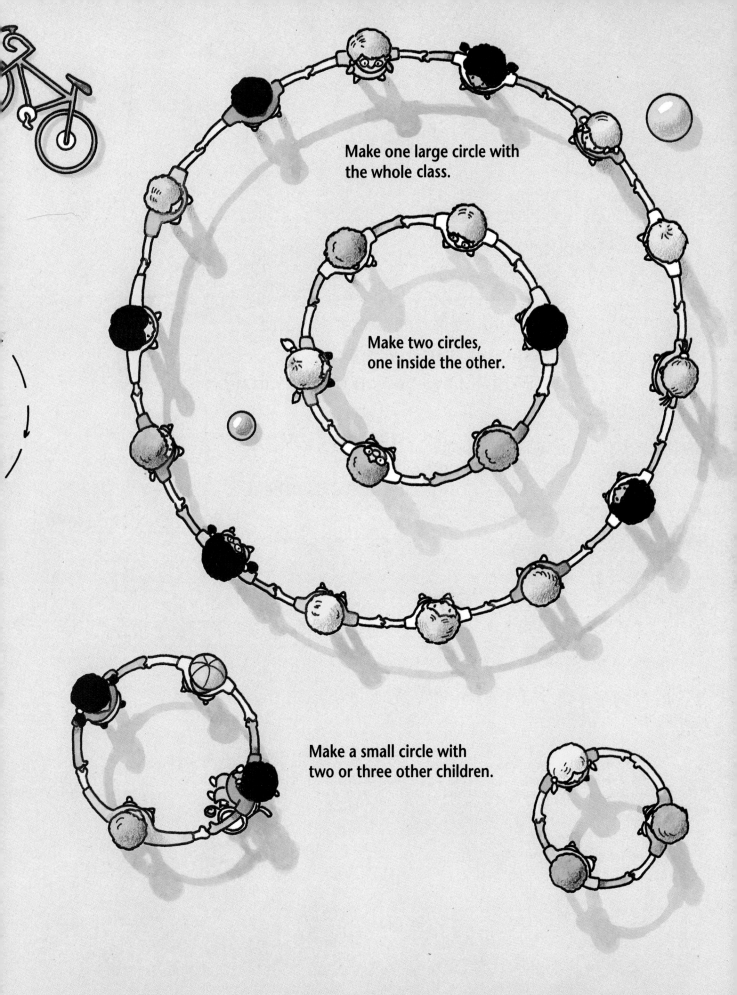

Make one large circle with
the whole class.

Make two circles,
one inside the other.

Make a small circle with
two or three other children.

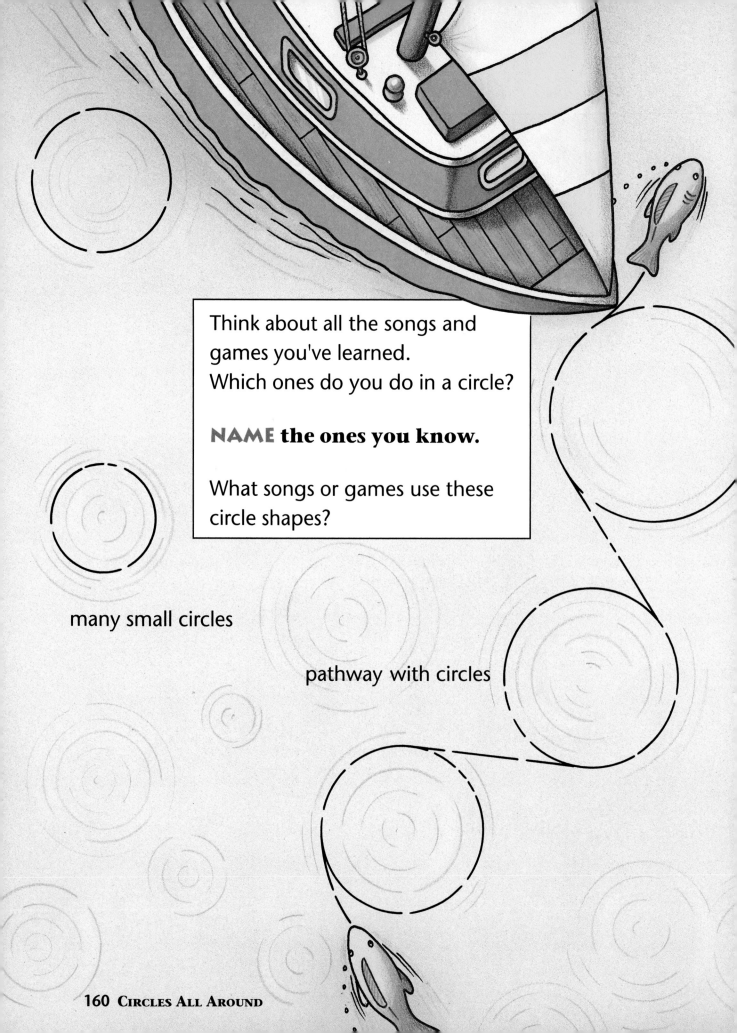

Think about all the songs and games you've learned.
Which ones do you do in a circle?

NAME the ones you know.

What songs or games use these circle shapes?

many small circles

pathway with circles

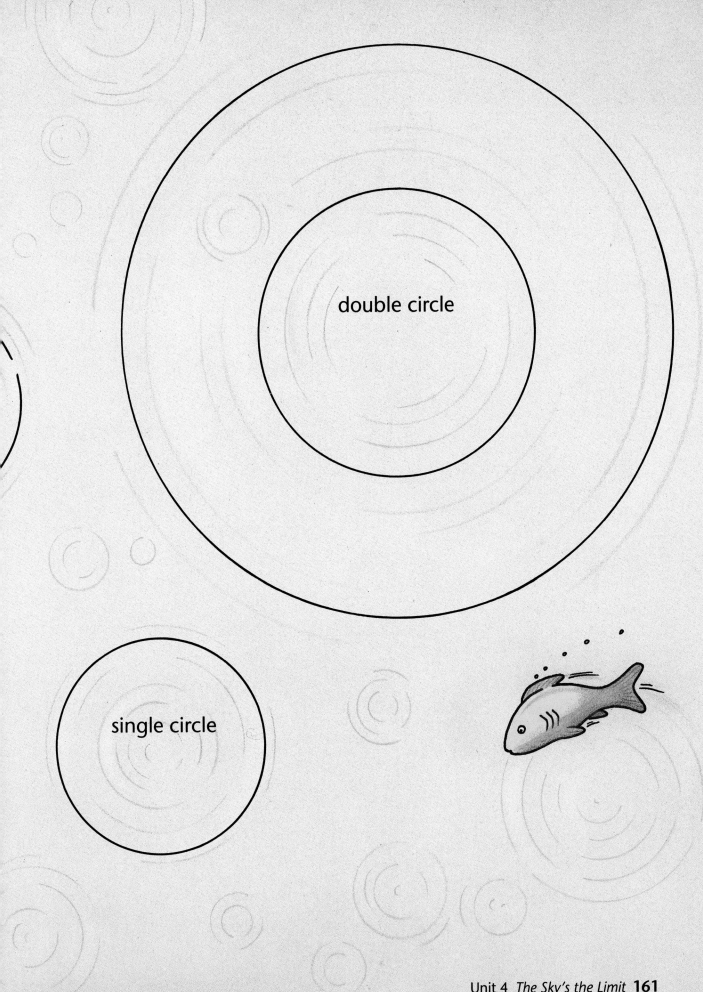

double circle

single circle

MY GREAT ADVENTURE

by Sally

Me

A spaceship landed in my yard. I got in! We flew around the sun, the moon, and the chimney pot.

We went to another planet. It had a nature park. We fed some purple acorns to an old squirrel.

← space trees

We saw a big city from outer space. It had very big skyscrapers!

We went to a baseball game in outer space. My favorite team won!

Home run! up in the stands!

Then we went home. Old Joe missed me. I told him all about my great adventure!

OLD JOE

1. Choose the rhythm you hear.

a.

b.

c.

2. Which rhythm do you hear?

a.

b.

c.

3. Which pitches do you hear?

a.

b.

c.

4. Choose the melody you hear.

a.

b.

c.

MAKE UP a melody and a dance to go with it!

Clap this rhythm until you know it well.

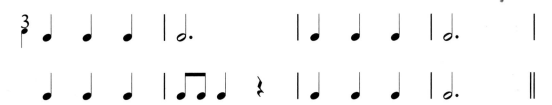

Add a melody using *mi re* and *do.*

CREATE a dance to go with your rhythm. Use steps that last one beat and steps that last three beats.

Your steps could have the same rhythm as your melody. Or you could choose to make up a new rhythm for the dance.

PLAY your melody with your dance.

Share

Write a letter to a pen pal. Tell about something you do in music class.

Write about it.   or      Draw a picture.

HORNS ARE

Pacific Islands

Africa

North America

A BLAST

People all over the world use many different materials to make horns.

LOOK at the instruments. What makes them the same? Different?

How do you think they would sound?

Australia

Europe

LISTENING

Montage of Horns

Listen to the different sounds of horns all over the world.

Accent on Surprise!

An old silent pond . . .
A frog jumps into the pond,

SPLASH!

Silence again.
—*Basho*

Loud, Soft, Action!

Here's a song that will really get you moving! You may be surprised at what you can do!

Learn these Spanish words.

SING and **MOVE** to "Mi cuerpo."

cuerpo = body

manos = hands

CLAP!

"cuerpo" doing the cha-cha-cha

pies = feet

Mi cuerpo

My Body

Hispanic Folk Song
English Version by MMH

Spanish: Mi cuer-po, mi cuer-po ha-ce mú-si - ca,
English: My bod-y makes mu-sic, it's eas-y, you will see,

Mi cuer-po, mi cuer-po ha-ce mú-si - ca.
My bod-y makes mu-sic, it's eas-y, you will see.

Mis ma-nos ha-cen (clap clap clap), mis
My hands, my hands go (clap clap clap), My

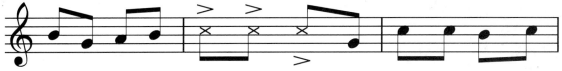

pi-es ha-cen (stamp stamp stamp), mi bo-ca ha-ce
feet, my feet go (stamp stamp stamp), My mouth, my mouth goes

"La la la," mi cuer-po ha-ce "Cha cha cha."
"La la la," My bod-y does the "Cha cha cha."

boca = mouth

This music may surprise you!

Russian Dance (Trepak)

from *The Nutcracker*

by Piotr Ilyich Tchaikovsky

Piotr Ilyich Tchaikovsky was a famous Russian composer. His ballet, **The Nutcracker,** *tells the story of a little girl's Christmas Eve dream.*

The Russian folk dance called the "Trepak" is one of many dances in The Nutcracker. *The dancers do high jumps and spins. The music gets suddenly louder when the dancers jump.*

Why do you think the dancers would make bigger movements with the louder sounds?

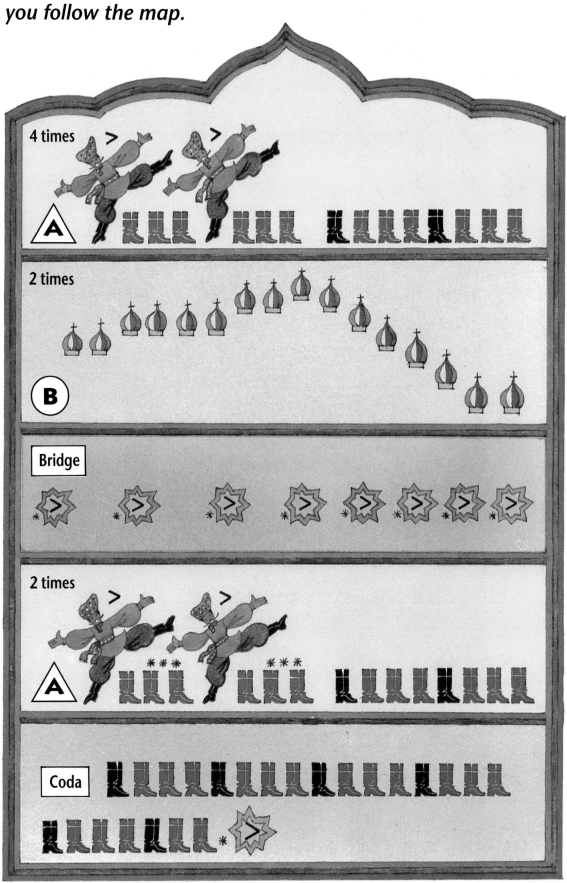

4 times

A

2 times

B

Bridge

2 times

A

Coda

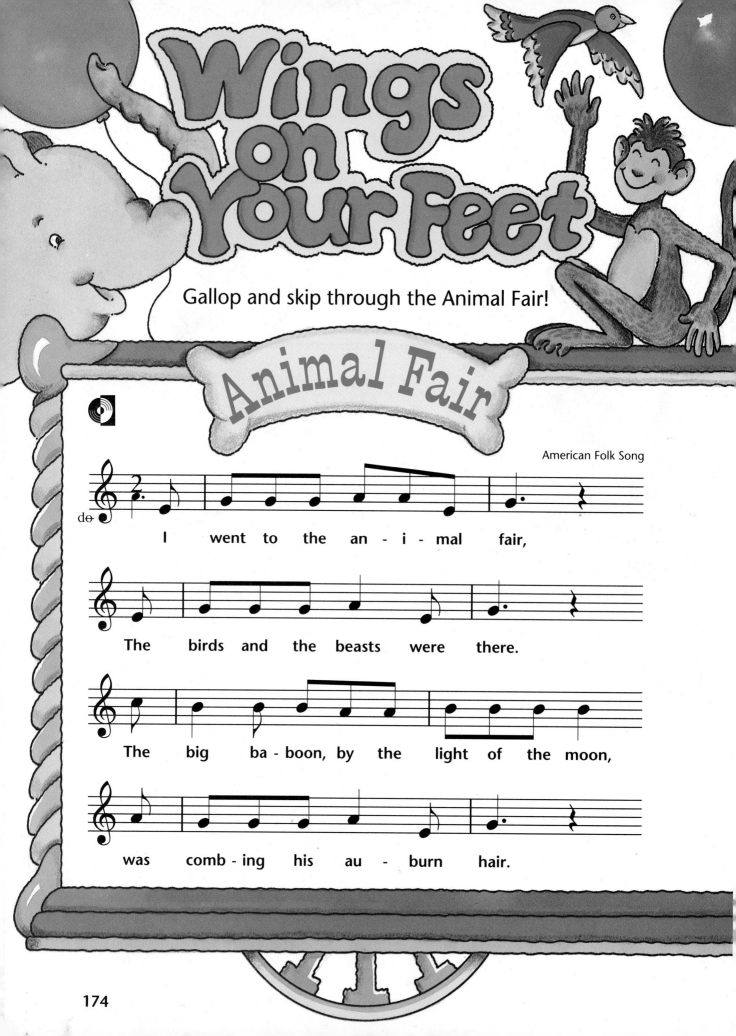

Wings on Your Feet

Gallop and skip through the Animal Fair!

Animal Fair

American Folk Song

I went to the an - i - mal fair,

The birds and the beasts were there.

The big ba - boon, by the light of the moon,

was comb - ing his au - burn hair.

174

You ought to have seen the monk;

He climbed up the el - e - phant's trunk.

The el - e - phant sneezed and fell on her knees,

and what be - came of the monk?

A TRIP AROUND THE RING

The animals you might see at a circus move in different ways.

When ponies trot around the ring, you hear two equal sounds on a beat.

When they gallop, you hear two unequal sounds on a beat. Which picture shows the trotting rhythm? The galloping rhythm?

LISTEN and **POINT** to the pattern
that matches the music you hear.

Which pattern also shows
a skipping rhythm?

ECHO to Double the FUN

This song tells a funny story. Listen and raise a hand when you hear the parts that repeat, or the **echo** parts. Then tell the story to a friend in your own words.

SING the echo parts of the song.

Bill Grogan's GOAT

American Folk Song

ECHO

There was a man →	There was a man
Now please take note	Now please take note
There was a man	There was a man
Who had a goat.	Who had a goat.
He loved that goat	He loved that goat
Indeed he did	Indeed he did
He loved that goat	He loved that goat
Just like a kid.	Just like a kid.

ECHO

One day the goat → One day the goat
Felt frisk and fine,   Felt frisk and fine,
Ate three red shirts   Ate three red shirts
Right off the line.   Right off the line.
The man, he grabbed   The man, he grabbed
Him by the back,   Him by the back,
And tied him to   And tied him to
A railroad track.   A railroad track.

ECHO

Now, when that train → Now, when that train
Hove into sight,   Hove into sight,
That goat grew pale   That goat grew pale
And green with fright,   And green with fright.
He heaved a sigh   He heaved a sigh
As if in pain,   As if in pain,
Coughed up the shirts   Coughed up the shirts
And flagged the train.   And flagged the train.

BE A COPYCAT!

When you do the same thing as someone else, you **imitate** them. Things you see or hear can have parts that are imitated. An echo is imitation that you hear.

TELL about the imitation you see here.

LISTENING

Gloria Patri

Long ago, this music was performed in huge churches. Musicians played the music from two different parts of the church. One group would play loudly. Then, from somewhere across the church, the other group would softly imitate the music.

Listen for the imitation in "Gloria Patri."

CREATE movements that show the imitation.

National Cathedral, Washington, D.C. Some stones used to build this church came from famous buildings around the world.

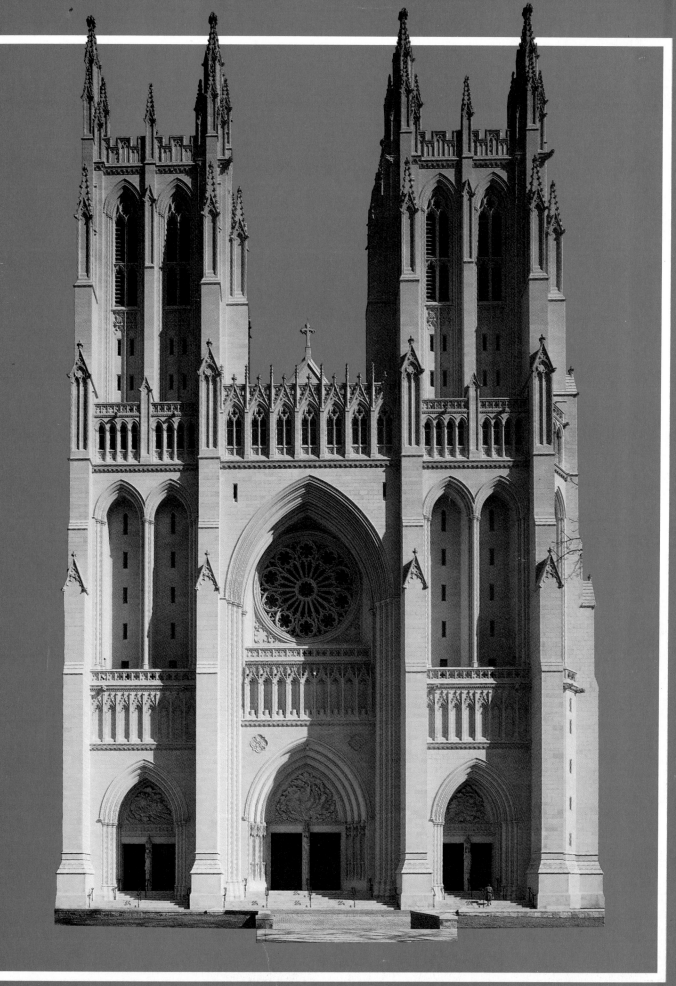

Some pictures have one part that catches your eye right away. That part might have a strong color or unusual shape. Something about it makes it stand out from the rest of the picture.

THE HEART
Henri Matisse cut out paper shapes to create this art.

The Heart. Plate 7 from *Jazz*.
The Metropolitan Museum of Art, Gift of Lila Acheson Wallace, 1983.
(1983.1009) (detail)

SOMETHING

Some sounds are stronger than others.

Say this part of "Bate, bate." Point to the words that sound stronger or louder.

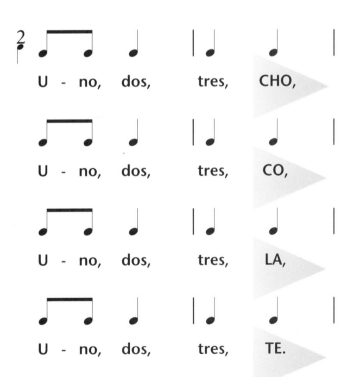

How can you tell that the sounds will be stronger?

MEET THE ACCENT

When you hear a note with an **accent,** it will sound stronger or louder. It will stand out from the other notes.

Find the accents in the music below.

Spanish: Mis ma - nos ha - cen (clap clap clap), mis pi - es ha - cen
English: My hands, my hands go (clap clap clap), My feet, my feet go

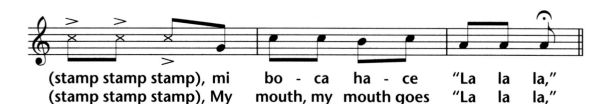

(stamp stamp stamp), mi bo - ca ha - ce "La la la,"
(stamp stamp stamp), My mouth, my mouth goes "La la la,"

SING the song. Make the notes with accents sound stronger.

READ the rhythm of this poem.

Say *frying* for ♫

Say *pan* for ♩

Now play the rhythm on instruments. Find the accents. Choose two special instruments to play them.

SPEAK, PLAY, and MOVE to "Two Little Sausages."

Two Little Sausages

American Rhyme

Two   lit - tle   sau - sa - ges

fry - ing   in   a   pan,

One   went   "Pop!"   and the

oth - er went   "Bam!"

RIDE INTO THE PAST

This African American song has been around for over 100 years. Can you imagine the sound of Uncle Jessie's horse and buggy as they go by? Listen for a trotting rhythm in the song.

African American Folk Song

'Long ___ come Un-cle Jes-sie, rid - ing through the fields

with ___ his horse and bug-gy and I know just how it feels.

Oh, _____ g'wan, girl, shake it,

g'wan, girl, shake it, g'wan, girl, shake it.

The trotting rhythm has two equal short sounds on each beat.

You can show two **equal sounds** to a beat this way.

This shows the sound your feet make when you trot.

The galloping and skipping rhythms have one long and one short sound on each beat.

You can show two **unequal sounds** this way.

This shows the sound your feet make when you skip or gallop.

Lou Pripet (French Folk Music)

This French song about a carpet maker is so old no one remembers who first made it up. It is played on a flute and a drum. One person plays both instruments.

LISTENING MAP *See if you can tell when the music changes from a skipping rhythm to a trotting rhythm.*

What tells you how many different sections the music has?

Which section has equal sounds?
♫

Unequal sounds?
♩♪

MOVE to show how the beats in each section are divided.

Fabricant de Tapis

la Musique

COPY CAT

When you copy what other people do, you imitate them. In "Bill Grogan's Goat," one part imitates the other.

Which color below shows the part that imitates?

Bill Grogan's Goat

American Folk Song

1. There was a man (there was a man)
2. One day the goat (one day the goat)

Now, please take note, (now, please take note)
Felt frisk and fine; (felt frisk and fine)

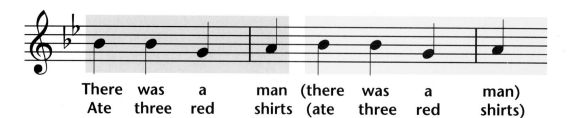

There was a man (there was a man)
Ate three red shirts (ate three red shirts)

Who had a goat. (who had a goat)
Right off the line. (right off the line)

COPY CAT

He   loved   that   goat,   (he   loved   that   goat)
The   man,   he   grabbed (the   man,   he   grabbed)

In - deed   he   did,   (in - deed   he   did)
Him   by   the   back,   (him   by   the   back)

He   loved   that   goat   (he   loved   that   goat)
And   tied   him   to   (and   tied   him   to)

Just   like   a   kid.   (just   like   a   kid)
A   rail - road   track.   (a   rail - road   track)

3. Now, when that train (now, when that train)
   Hove into sight, (hove into sight)
   That goat grew pale (that goat grew pale)
   And green with fright, (and green with fright)
   He heaved a sigh, (he heaved a sigh)
   As if in pain; (as if in pain)
   Coughed up the shirts (coughed up the shirts)
   And flagged the train. (and flagged the train)

IMITATE TO LEARN A SONG

There are many ways to learn a new song. Learn
this one by echoing the pitch syllables you hear.
Then pretend to take a ride in a buggy while
you sing.

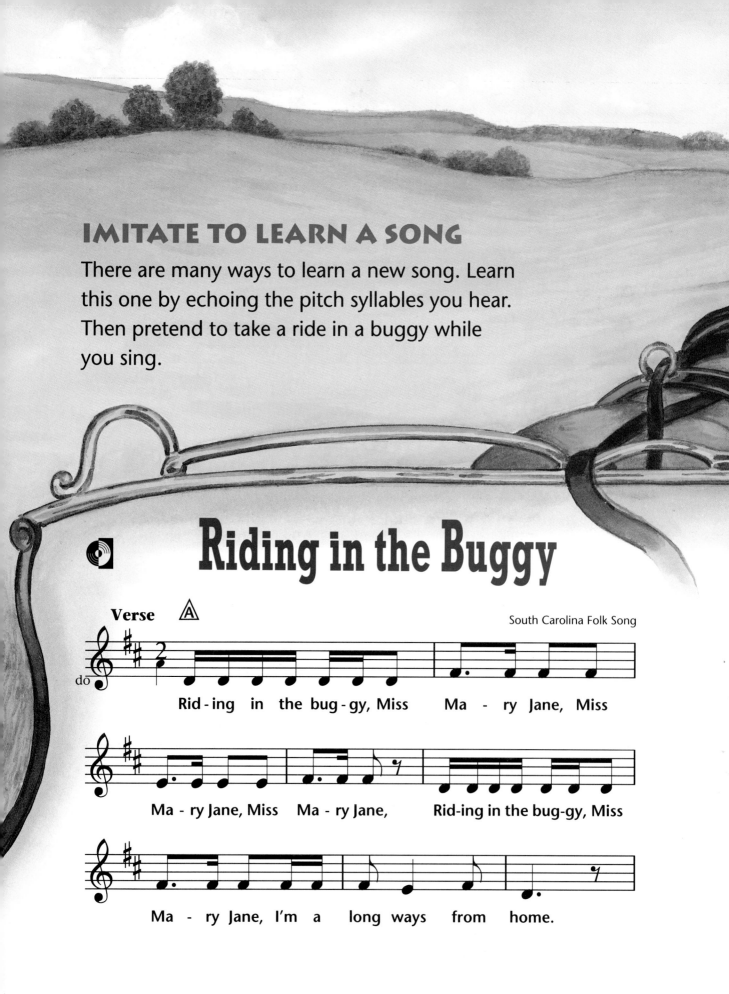

Riding in the Buggy

Verse Ⓐ

South Carolina Folk Song

Rid-ing in the bug-gy, Miss   Ma - ry Jane, Miss

Ma - ry Jane, Miss   Ma - ry Jane,   Rid-ing in the bug-gy, Miss

Ma - ry Jane, I'm a   long ways   from   home.

Refrain
Ⓑ

Who moan for me? Who moan for me?

Who moan for me, my dar-ling, Who moan for me?

BRASS

INSTRUMENTS TAKE A BOW

Brass instruments can always get your attention. They're hard not to notice, whether you're looking at them or listening to them!

You have heard these instruments many times this year.

French horn

Read the name of each instrument.

POINT to each instrument as you
hear it played.

trombone

trumpet

tuba

BRASS WITH A FRENCH TWIST

Although this song is from France, the melody is sung in many other countries.

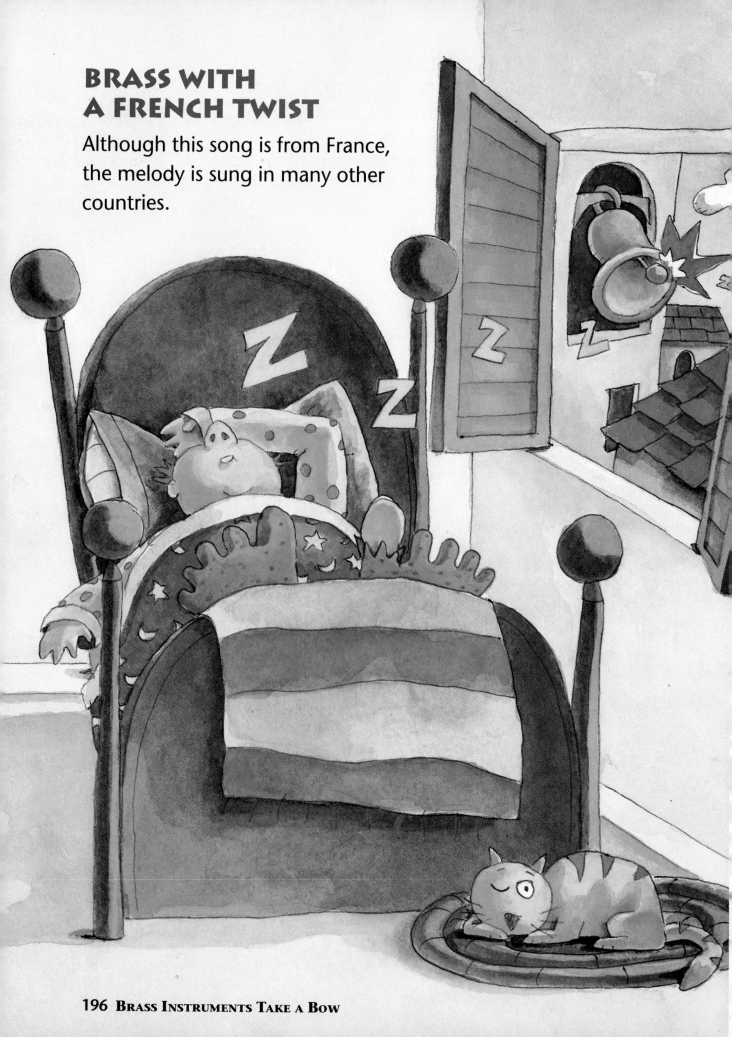

You can sing "Frère Jacques" in French and in English.

LISTEN for the brass instruments in this song.

Frère Jacques

Are You Sleeping?

French Folk Song

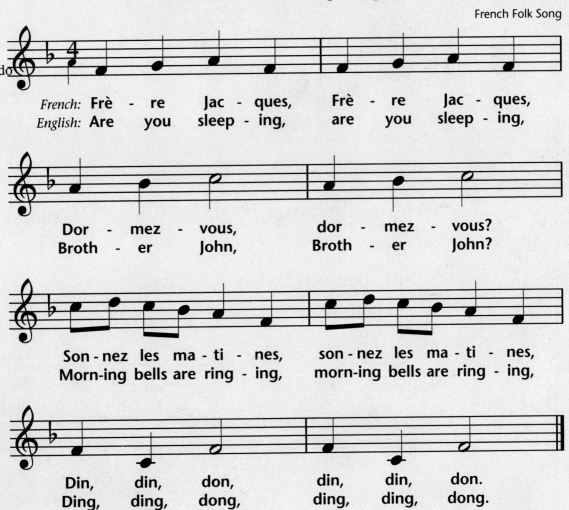

French: **Frè - re Jac - ques, Frè - re Jac - ques,**
English: **Are you sleep - ing, are you sleep - ing,**

Dor - mez - vous, dor - mez - vous?
Broth - er John, Broth - er John?

Son - nez les ma - ti - nes, son - nez les ma - ti - nes,
Morn-ing bells are ring - ing, morn-ing bells are ring - ing,

Din, din, don, din, din, don.
Ding, ding, dong, ding, ding, dong.

Musical PUZZLES

Use what you know about melody and rhythm to solve some musical puzzles!

POINT to *do re* and *mi.*

The music below has only note heads. What's missing?

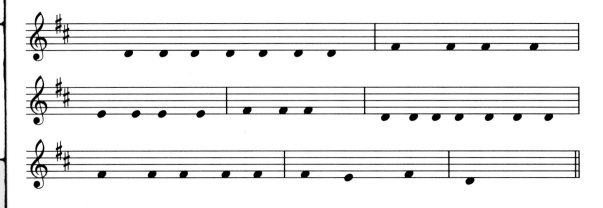

PAT this pattern on your knees with
" 'Long Come Uncle Jessie."

left right left right left right left right

Make a trotting sound in different
ways. Play the pattern on temple
blocks or use paper cups.

PLAY this part on a
pitched instrument.

Which notes show *do*? *re*?

left right left right left right left right

SOMETHING OLD, SOMETHING NEW

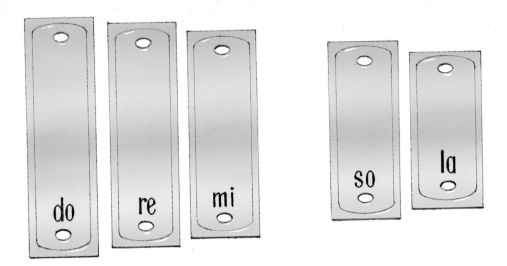

CREATE a new melody using *do re mi so* and *la*.
Choose pitches to play with the rhythm
of "Frère Jacques."

Divide into two groups.

Group 1: Clap and play the orange parts.

Group 2: Clap and play the blue parts.

VISIT THE ANIMAL FAIR!

You're off to the animal fair! Sometimes your balloon pops! In music, what would a single loud sound be called?

Stop and eat breakfast. The animals are serving sausages.

Look! It's an animal parade! Are the animals trotting or galloping? How can you tell?

The animals have invited you to join them! Will you trot or gallop to the music?

CHECK IT OUT

1. Listen to a pattern with an accented sound. Choose the sign that needs to be added to show that the sound is suddenly louder.

   a. ♩   **b.** ◁═   **c.** :‖   **d.** >

2. Point to the beat in this rhythm where you hear an accent.

3. How would you move to this music?
   a. trot
   b. gallop

4. What do you hear?
   a. music with equal sounds
   b. music with unequal sounds

CREATE

Sometimes a poem or story suggests sounds.

> Froggy Boggy
> tried to jump
> on a stone
> and got a bump.
>
> It made his eyes
> wink and frown
> and turned his nose
> upside down.
> —*Anonymous*

1. Tell the poem's story in your own words. What sounds might you hear?

2. Choose instruments for your sounds. Which sounds might need an accent?

3. Tell the story with sounds only—no words! Use a few accented sounds at important moments.

4. Perform your piece for the class.

Share

Make up a new animal. What will it look like? What sound will it make?

| Write about your animal. | or | Draw your animal. |

The Weaver's World

Cloth is made by weaving threads together.

LOOK at your clothes. Can you see the threads that are woven?

To make cloth, a weaver begins with a raw material. One choice is cotton.

The raw material is spun into thread or yarn. The spinning tool is called a *weasel*. The weasel pulls the thread. It pops up when the thread is ready.

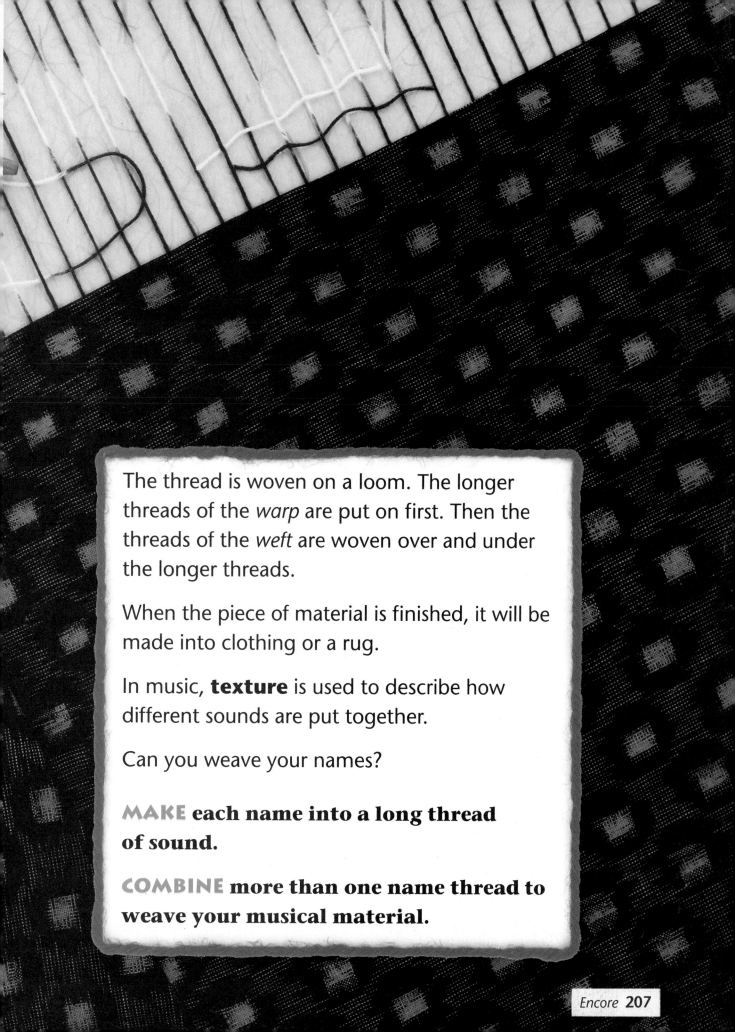

The thread is woven on a loom. The longer threads of the *warp* are put on first. Then the threads of the *weft* are woven over and under the longer threads.

When the piece of material is finished, it will be made into clothing or a rug.

In music, **texture** is used to describe how different sounds are put together.

Can you weave your names?

MAKE each name into a long thread of sound.

COMBINE more than one name thread to weave your musical material.

THE SPIDER WEAVER

A Folk Tale from Japan

Once there was a farmer named Yosaku. One day he saw a snake ready to eat a spider. He chased the snake away, saving the spider's life.

A few days later, a young girl came to Yosaku's house looking for work. Yosaku hired her to weave some cloth. By the end of the day, she had woven enough cloth to make eight kimonos!

"How ever did you weave so much?" Yosaku asked. "I can't tell you," the girl said. "But you must never come into my weaving room." The next day Yosaku peeped in the window and saw a spider weaving very fast. Then Yosaku understood. The girl was really the spider he had saved. It had come back to thank Yosaku by weaving him some cloth.

One day, Yosaku went to a nearby village and bought a new bundle of cotton. On the way home, he stopped to rest. The snake that had tried to eat the spider crept into the bundle.

Yosaku arrived home and gave the bundle to the girl. She turned into a spider so she could weave some more cloth. Then the snake jumped out, and the frightened spider ran away. The snake caught the spider and prepared to eat it.

In the sky, Old Man Sun had been watching. He reached down with a sunbeam, lifting the spider high into the sky, safe from the snake.

The spider was so grateful that it wove beautiful cottony clouds in the sky. Some say that's why clouds look like cotton, and both the spider and the cloud have the same name in Japan–*kumo*.

CHOOSE **an instrument sound for each character. Then perform the story.**

UNIT 6

IMAGINE . . .

Johnny

To Johnny a box
is a house
or a car
or a ship
or a train
or a horse.
A stick is a sword
or a spear
or a cane,
and a carpet
is magic,
of course.

　　　　—Marci Ridlon

Up, Up, and Away

Music can be a kind of magic carpet.
It can take you many places in your imagination!

LISTENING

MEET CHARNELE BROWN

Charnele Brown is an actress who grew up in a musical family. Listen as she tells about some favorite music. The songs took her traveling to imaginary places.

OCEAN

Name the places you see here.

MATCH the rhythm of each place to a note.

ZOO

PARK

Someone is tapping at the window!

Who's That Tapping at the Window?

American Singing Game

Who's   that   tap-ping   at   the   win - dow?

Who's   that   knock-ing   at   the   door?

I   am   tap-ping   at   the   win - dow.

I   am   knock-ing   at   the   door.

Find these notes or rests in the song.

READ each rhythm. Choose a different word to say for each note.

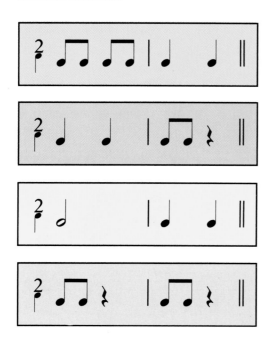

Now clap this rhythm. It was made from two shorter rhythms above. Which ones were used?

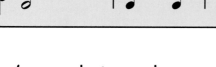

You're ready to make up your own rhythm! Choose two lines above. Put them together to make a longer rhythm.

PLAY your rhythm on an unpitched instrument.

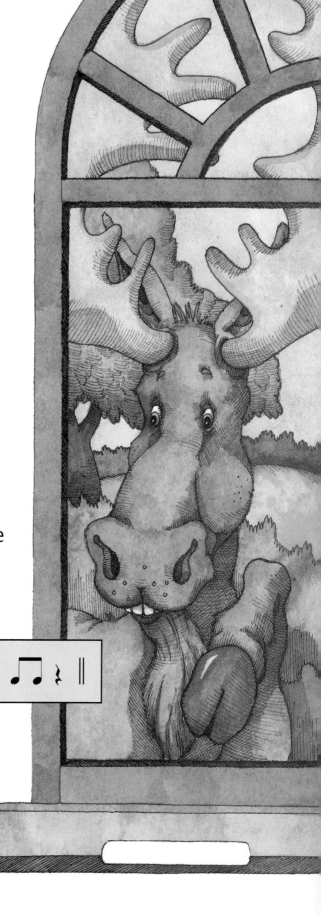

Over and Over

Next stop on the flying carpet trip–the zoo!

Goin' to the Zoo

Words and Music by Tom Paxton

Verse

1. Dad-dy's tak-in' us to the zoo to-mor-row, ___
2. See the el-e-phant with the long trunk swing-in', ___

zoo to-mor-row, ___ zoo to-mor-row, ___
Great big ears and ___ long trunk swing-in', ___

Dad-dy's tak-in' us to the zoo to-mor-row, ___
Sniff-in' up ___ pea-nuts with the long trunk swing-in', ___

We can ___ stay all day.
We can ___ stay all day.

216

We're go - in' to the zoo, zoo, zoo.

How a - bout you, you, you?

You can come too, too, too.

We're go - in' to the zoo, zoo, zoo. zoo.

3. See all the monkeys scritch,
      scritch, scratchin',
   Jumpin' round scritch, scritch,
      scratchin',
   Hangin' by their long tails,
      scritch, scritch, scratchin',
   We can stay all day. *Refrain*

4. Big black bear all huff-a-puffin',
   Coat's too heavy, he's a-puffin,
   Don't get too near the
      huff-a-puffin',
   You can't stay all day. *Refrain*

5. Seals in the pool all honk, honk,
      honkin',
   Catchin' fish, and honk, honk,
      honkin',
   Little seals all honk, honk,
      honkin',
   We can stay all day. *Refrain*

6. We stayed all day, and I'm gettin'
      sleepy,
   Gettin' sleepy, gettin' sleepy,
   Home already and I'm sleep,
      sleep, sleepy,
   We have stayed all day. *Refrain*

SHAPES MAKE FORMS

This picture has many shapes you know.
Look for the circles, squares, and triangles.

FIND the shapes that are used more
than once.

COLORED RHYTHM NO. 698

Sonia Delaunay used colored shapes in this
painting. Why do you think she named it
Colored Rhythm?

Contre-danse

from *Les Indes galantes*
by Jean Philippe Rameau

LISTEN for the section that you hear more than once. Choose a way to move each time you hear that section.

Musicians sometimes use letters to show the form of a song.

Use the letter A for the first shape.
Use a new letter for each new shape.
If a shape repeats, use the same letter for it as you used before.

SAY the letters that go with these shapes.

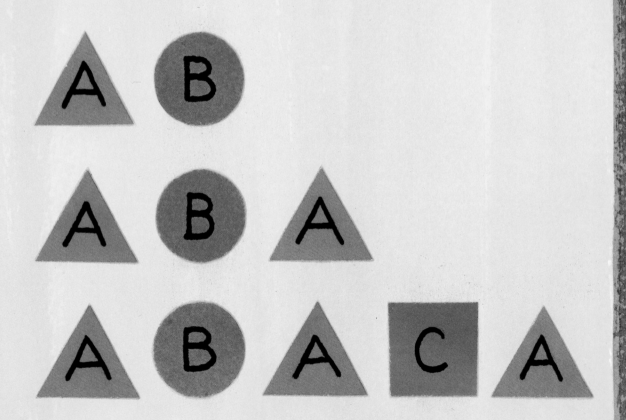

Sing a Line, Dance a Line

How do you **sashay**? What is an **elbow swing**? Do a dance and find out!

FOLLOW the "head couple." They show the steps of the dance.

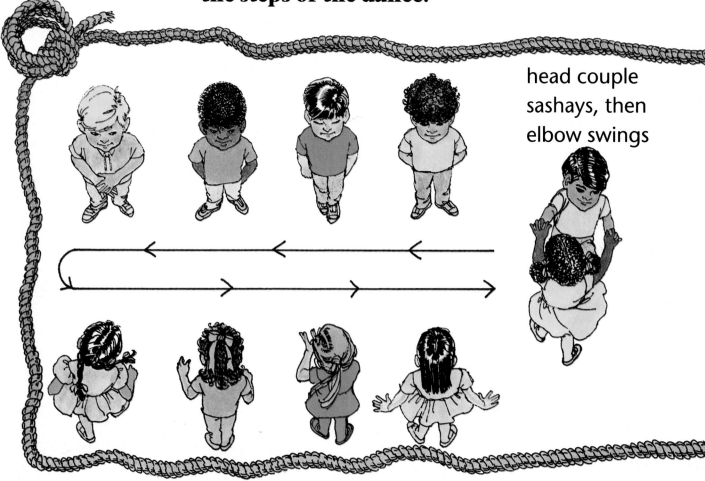

head couple sashays, then elbow swings

This Alabama song was popular in the days of one-room schoolhouses. Children would dance and sing it at recess. Today people still have fun singing it at country dances.

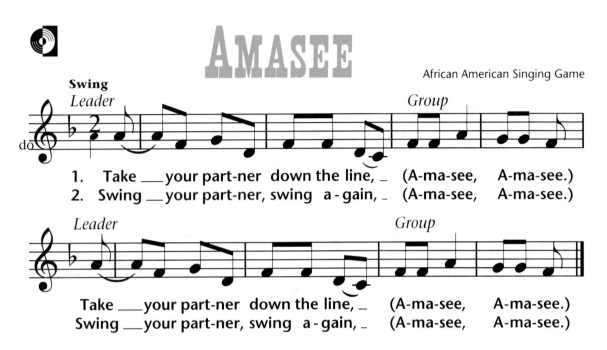

AMASEE

African American Singing Game

1. Take ___ your part-ner down the line, _ (A-ma-see, A-ma-see.)
2. Swing ___ your part-ner, swing a-gain, _ (A-ma-see, A-ma-see.)

Take ___ your part-ner down the line, _ (A-ma-see, A-ma-see.)
Swing ___ your part-ner, swing a-gain, _ (A-ma-see, A-ma-see.)

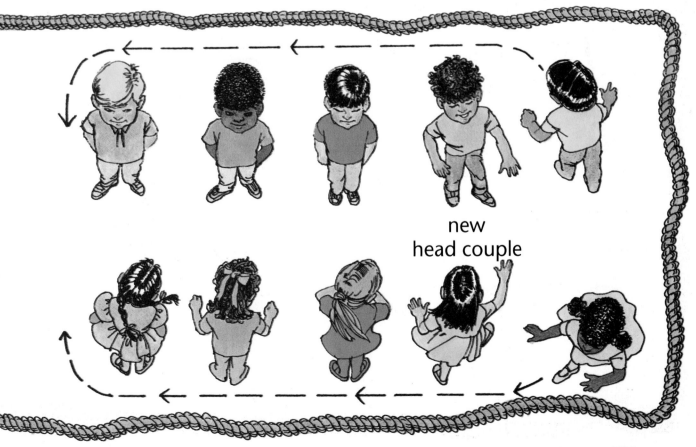

new
head couple

Listen to this Spanish song. Think about how you might move to the music.

A LA PUERTA DEL CIELO

At the Gate of Heaven

Spanish Folk Song
English Version by MMH

Spanish: A la puer-ta del cie-lo ven-den za-pa-tos,
English: At the gate of Heav'n they are sell-ing *za-pa-tos,*

Pa-ra los an-ge-li-tos que an-dan des-cal-zos.
For the lit-tle an-gels who go walk-ing bare-foot.

Duér-me-te, ni-ño, duér-me-te, ni-ño,
Slum-ber my ba-by, slum-ber my ba-by,

Duér-me-te, ni-ño, a-rru, a-rru.
slum-ber my ba-by, a-rru, a-rru.

CREATE a dance for the song. Which lines have the same melody?

Choose a movement to make when you hear the same melody.
Choose a different movement to make when you hear a different melody.

RHYMES TO GO

You've made up rhythms, melodies, and dances.
This song asks you to make up a rhyme.

READ these pitches. Then find them in
the song below.

MAKE
UP A
RHYME

American Playground Song
As Sung by Margaret Campbelle-duGard

Make up a rhyme and say it on time and throw it out the win-dow.

Make up a rhyme and say it on time and throw it out the win-dow, __

the win-dow, __the win-dow, __the se-cond stor-y win-dow.

Make up a rhyme and say it on time and throw it out the win-dow.

LISTEN to these rhymes.
They begin with words you know.
The ending will surprise you.

Mistress Mary, quite contrary,
How does your garden grow?
With silver bells, and cockle shells,
And throw them out the window!
The window, the window . . .

Humpty Dumpty sat on the wall.
Humpty Dumpty had a great fall.
All the king's horses and all the king's men
Just threw him out the window!
The window, the window . . .

Ride your flying carpet out the window to Hawaii.
You can see many beautiful fish there.

MY FISH
KU'U I'A

1. My fish, he has a mouth, see, now, here it is.
   He eats with his mouth.

Refrain:
   Auē nō ho'i ē!
   Holo aku holo mai.
   My fish, he is a good fish, living in the sea.

2. My fish, he has some gills, see, now, here they are.
   He opens them and closes them.

3. My fish, he has some fins, see, now, here they are.
   He swims with his fins.

4. My fish, he has a dorsal fin, see, now, here it is.
   He waves with his dorsal fin.

5. My fish, he has a tail, see, now, here it is.
   He swishes with his tail.

What parts of a fish can you name?

Read this pattern.

How many times do you hear it in "Ku'u I'a"?

KU'U I'A
MY FISH

Words and Music by 'Aha Pūnana Leo
English Version by MMH

Verse

Hawaiian: He nu-ku ko ka i -'a ei - a ma 'a - ne 'i.
English: My fish, he has a mouth, __ see, now, here it is. He

'Ai kā - na ha - na.
eats with his mouth. ____

Refrain

Au __ ē nō ho -'i ē! __ Ho - lo a - ku ho - lo mai.

He i -'a ma - i - ka -'i no - ho ma ke kai.
My fish, he is a good fish, liv - ing in the sea.

CREATE a melody for the third line.

RONDO!

You know how to use different shapes to show a musical form. Some forms are used so often in music, they have special names.

Here are the sections of "Contre-danse."

A B A C A D A E A F A

The A section is heard several times. Other sections come between, but the A section always returns. This form is called a **rondo.**

LISTEN to "Contre-danse" **and follow the form.**

MOVE TO A RONDO

Some movements let you follow a
pathway. Other movements keep
you in one place.

**CREATE a movement
for each section of
"Contre-danse."**

Follow a pathway for the A
sections. Do the same
movement when you
hear it.

Stay in one place for the
other sections. Do different
movements for each of them.

A CLASS RONDO

Now's your chance to create a rondo with your class.

CREATE a melody for a poem. Work in groups. Each group's melody will be a different section to play between the A sections of your rondo.

Choose a poem and say it together.

Decide what rhythm to use with the words.

Change the ending of the poem to "throw it out the window."

Make up a *do re mi so la* melody for your rhyme. Use F G A C D.

Practice saying and playing your rhyme.

If all the world was apple pie,
And all the sea was ink,
And all the trees were bread and cheese,
What would we have to drink?

—*Mother Goose*

Old bull moose who dreamed he could fly
Sailed across a starry sky.
But when daylight came he was up a tree:
A peculiar place for a moose to be!

—*Alaska Mother Goose*

Humpty Dumpty sat on a wall.
At three o'clock, he had his great fall.
The king set the time machine back to two.
Now Humpty's unscrambled and good as new.

—*Space Age Mother Goose*

Put it all together! Sing the first part of "Make Up a Rhyme" for your A section. Then use each group's melody as the B and C sections of your rondo.

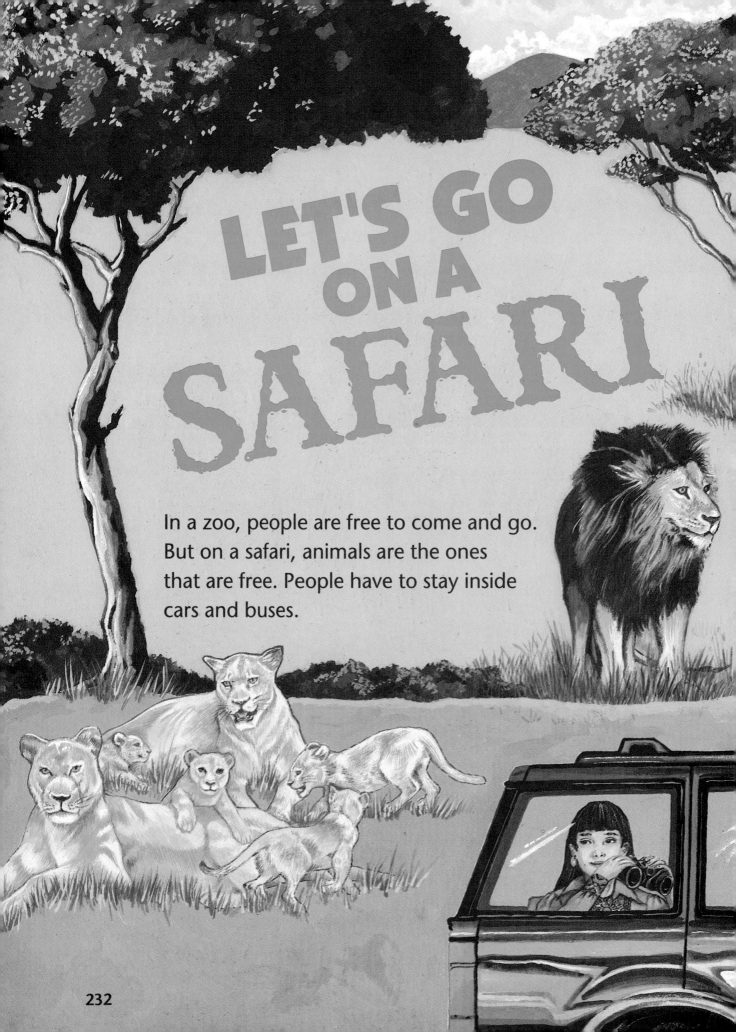

LET'S GO ON A SAFARI

In a zoo, people are free to come and go. But on a safari, animals are the ones that are free. People have to stay inside cars and buses.

When a part is repeated, or echoed, it's called *imitation*. Where do you see and hear imitation below?

Solo:

Look outside and what do I see?

Group:

Look outside and what do I see?

Solo:

I see a _____ looking at me!

Group:

I see a _____ looking at me!

Animals roam freely in special African parks. The road signs there say *pole.* That means "go slow" in Swahili. The signs remind people to drive carefully and watch out for the animals.

SPOTLIGHT ON ELLA JENKINS

Ella Jenkins is a popular composer and singer. She travels all over the world sharing her music. She has taught her songs to children in many countries. Ms. Jenkins wrote "Pole, Pole" after visiting an animal park in Kenya.

POLE, POLE

Leader   *Group*   Words and Music by Ella Jenkins

Swahili/English: **Po – le, po – le,**   *(po – le, po – le,)*

go slow, go slow, ___   *(go slow, go slow,)* ___

po – le, po – le,   *(po – le, po – le,)*

That's where the an - i - mals go.   *(That's where the an - i - mals go.)*

B

Solo: Look outside and what do I see?
Group: Look outside and what do I see?
Solo: I see a _____ looking at me!
Group: I see a _____ looking at me!

**FIND the imitation in the A section
of "Pole, Pole."**

POLE

These pictures show a very special kind of imitation. Try it out!

Group 1: Follow the words in the green boxes.
Group 2: Follow the words in the yellow boxes.
Group 2 begins to imitate Group 1 after four beats. It doesn't wait until Group 1 finishes.

Group 1	Look outside and	what do I see?

Group 2	Look outside and

This kind of imitation has a special name–a **canon.**

| I see a _____ | looking at me! | |
| what do I see? | I see a _____ | looking at me! |

THINK IT THROUGH
Explain how a canon is the same as imitation.
Tell how it is different from imitation.

A CITY OF Clocks

Fly your carpet to the city of Vienna, Austria. It is famous for its music and musicians. The clockmakers of Vienna are also famous. Their clocks have little wooden dancers or animals that move when the clock strikes.

LISTENING

Viennese Musical Clock
from *Háry János Suite*
by *Zoltán Kodály*

LISTENING MAP
Follow the map as you listen.

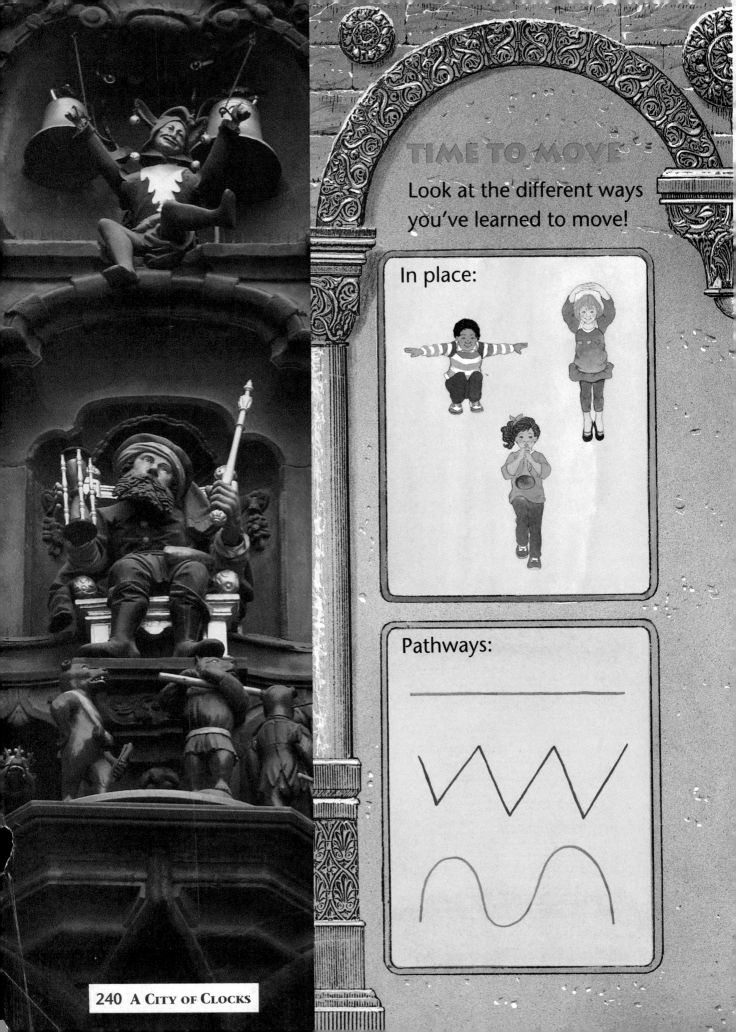

TIME TO MOVE

Look at the different ways you've learned to move!

In place:

Pathways:

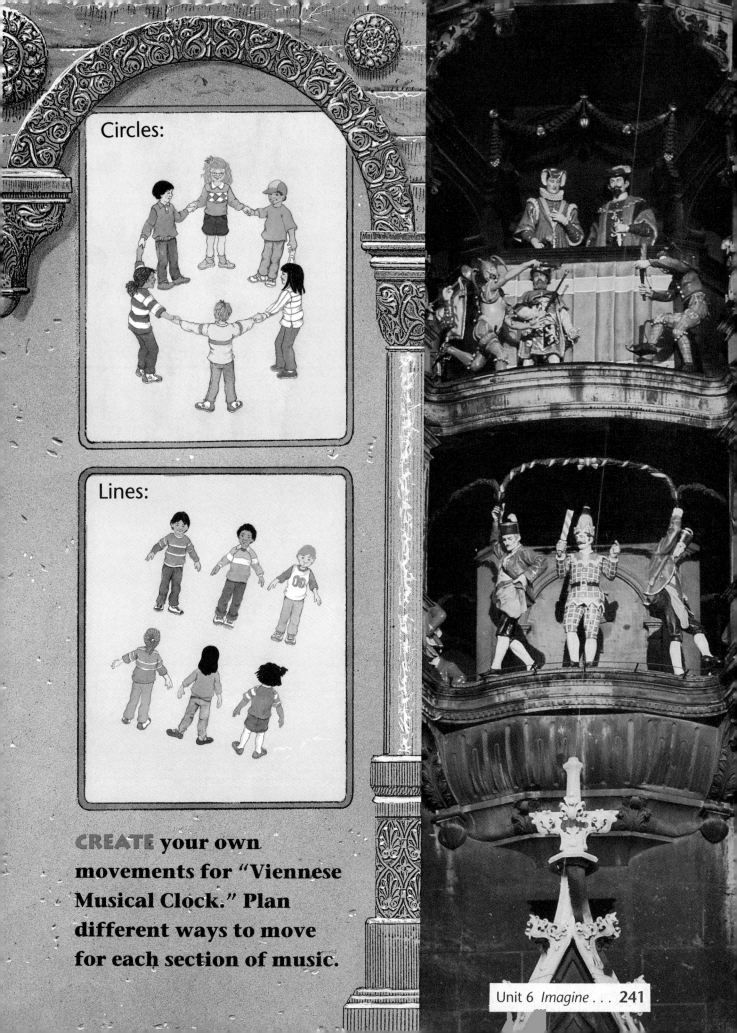

Circles:

Lines:

CREATE your own movements for "Viennese Musical Clock." Plan different ways to move for each section of music.

Help! The words for this song are missing! Can you discover what song it is?

USE these clues to find out what song it is.

Read the rhythm.
Read the pitches.
Put the rhythm and pitches
together to solve the mystery.

Well done! You've solved the mystery!

PLAY the melody. Use the letter names below each pitch.

do F *re* G *mi* A *so* C

WHICH SONG IS WHICH?

Can you solve another musical mystery? This time there is music for "Goin' to the Zoo" and "Ku'u i'a," but–oh, no!–the words are missing again! See if you can decide which song is which.

PLAY one of these patterns on an instrument.

YOU DID IT!

You solved another musical mystery. What clues did you use? What happened when you put them all together? Congratulations–you are reading music!

REVIEW

TO THE ZOO

Take a trip to the zoo! Hurry and catch the bus!

Do you know any songs that use ABA form?

What rhythms do
you see?

ZOO

PARK

OCEAN

Round up your
trip with a rondo!

RONDO

CHECK IT OUT

1. Which form do you hear?

   a. A A   **b.** A B   **c.** rondo form   **d.** A B A

---

2. Which rhythm pattern do you hear?

   a. (rhythm notation)

   b. (rhythm notation)

   c. (rhythm notation)

---

3. Choose the rhythm you hear.

   a. (rhythm notation)

   b. (rhythm notation)

   c. (rhythm notation)

---

4. Choose the form you hear.

   a. A B   **b.** A B A   **c.** rondo   **d.** something else

CREATE

MAKE a zoo rondo.

List some animals and some movements.

Match the first letter of an animal name with the first letter of a movement.

twisting tigers

rolling rhinos

hopping hippos

Show your animal's movement. Use movements that are long ♩ medium ♪ ♪ or short and quick ♫ ♫

Add instrument sounds.

Create a rondo. For the A sections, sing the refrain of "Goin' to the Zoo." For the other sections, do your animal movements.

Share

Imagine that the flying carpet has taken you somewhere. Close your eyes and listen closely. Can you tell where you are by the sounds you hear?

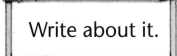

Write about it.   or   Draw a picture.

WE'RE A TEAM

A band is like a team. Each person on the team has a job. Everybody works together.

A **conductor** helps the band play together.

MEET
Paula Crider

Paula Crider is a band conductor. Listen as she tells about her job.

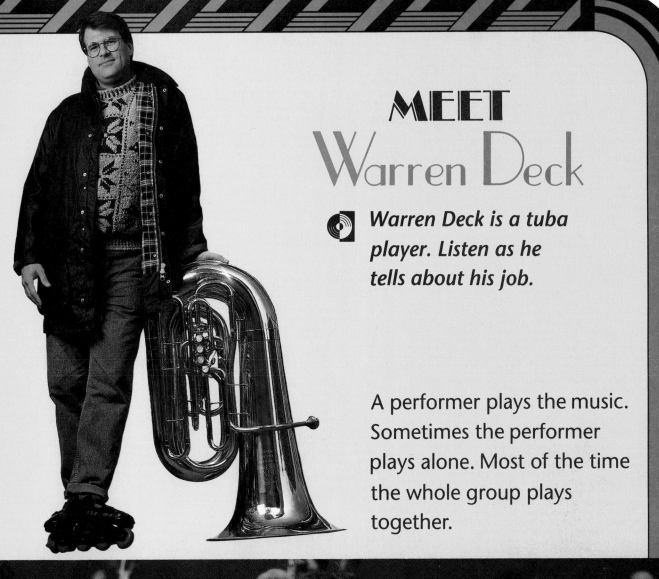

MEET

Warren Deck

Warren Deck is a tuba player. Listen as he tells about his job.

A performer plays the music. Sometimes the performer plays alone. Most of the time the whole group plays together.

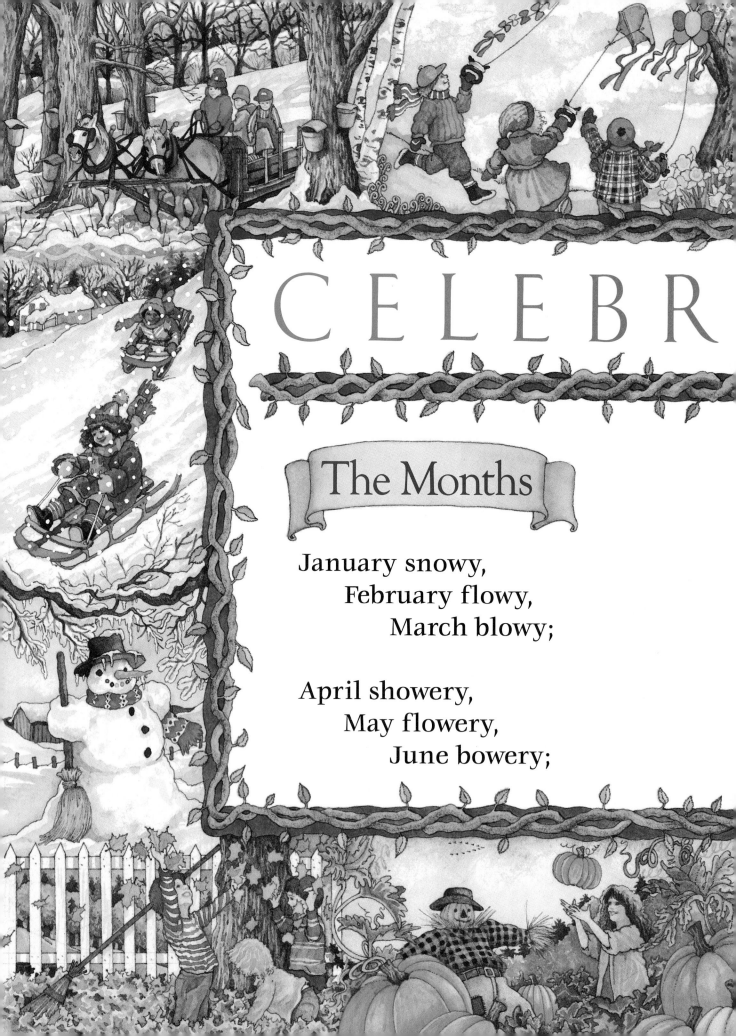

CELEBR

The Months

January snowy,
February flowy,
March blowy;

April showery,
May flowery,
June bowery;

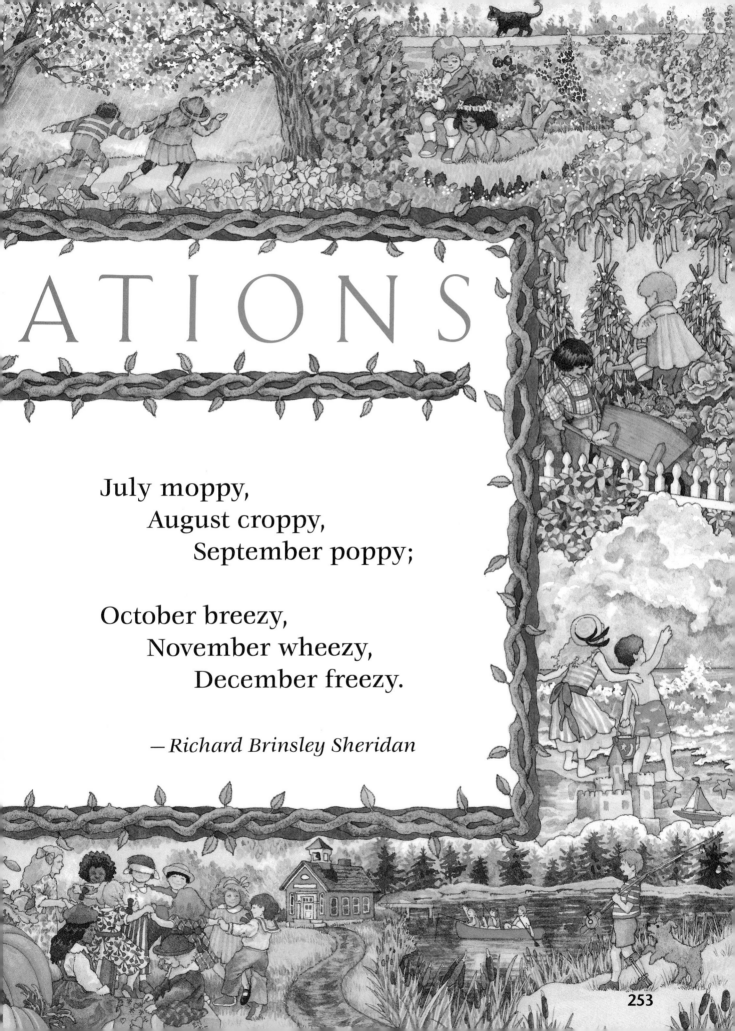

ATIONS

July moppy,
    August croppy,
        September poppy;

October breezy,
    November wheezy,
        December freezy.

— *Richard Brinsley Sheridan*

The Land of Liberty

AMERICA

Music by Henry Carey
Words by Samuel F. Smith

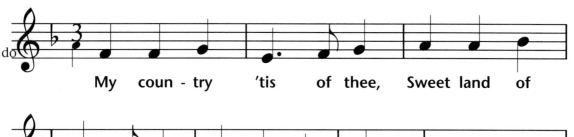

My coun - try 'tis of thee, Sweet land of

lib - er - ty, Of thee I sing. Land where my

fa - thers died, Land of the Pil - grim's pride,

From ev' - ry __ moun-tain-side Let __ free-dom ring.

This Land Is Your Land

Words and Music by Woody Guthrie

This land is your land, ___ This land is my land, ___

From Cal - i - for - nia ___ to the New York is - land, ___

From the red-wood for - est ___ to the Gulf Stream wa - ters; ___

This land was made for you and me. ___

YANKEE DOODLE

Traditional Melody
Words by Dr. Richard Shuckburgh

Verse

1. Fath'r and I went down to camp
2. Yan - kee Doo - dle went to camp town,

a - long with Cap - tain Good - in',
a - rid - ing on a po - ny,

and there we saw the men and boys
He stuck a feath - er in his cap

as thick as hast - y pud - din'.
and called it mac - a - ro - ni.

Refrain

Yan-kee Doo-dle keep it up, Yan-kee Doo-dle dan - dy,

Mind the mu-sic and the step, and with the girls be han - dy.

3. There was Captain Washington upon a slapping stallion,
   a-giving orders to his men; I guess there were a million.

WHEN THE FLAG GOES BY

Words and Music by Lynn Freeman Olson

1. When the flag goes by, hold it high!
2. When you hear this song, sing out strong!

Wave it for our coun - try!
Sing it for our coun - try!

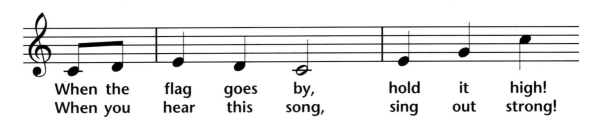

When the flag goes by, hold it high!
When you hear this song, sing out strong!

And cheer when the flag goes by!
And cheer when the flag goes by!

Why do you think countries have flags?

Spooky Night

Have you ever been afraid of something that wasn't even there? What was it?

The **THING** That Isn't There

Words and Music by Tom Paxton

1. and 7. I'll tell you what I tru-ly fear,
(2.) is - n't un-der my broth-er's bed,

What gives me the wool-i-est scare, _____
It is - n't be-hind ____ the chair. _____

I'll tell you what I dread the most:
It's hard to say just where it is:

The thing that is - n't there.

1.–6. Hoo ooh. _____ 2. It **7.** ooh! _____

3. And when my mother turns out the light,
   I lie in my bed and stare.
   I stare at the wall prepared to see
   The thing that isn't there.

4. It wasn't there for weeks and weeks,
   So I took extra care.
   It gives me the creeps to think of it:
   The thing that isn't there.

5. And now on a dark and stormy night,
   I bravely climb the stairs,
   And open the closet door to face
   The thing that isn't there.

6. It isn't there again tonight.
   The prickles in my hair
   Inform me that I'm very near to
   The thing that isn't there.

Someone

Someone came knocking
    At my wee, small door,
Someone came knocking,
    I'm sure—sure—sure;
I listened, I opened,
    I looked to left and right,
But nought there was a-stirring
    In the still dark night.
Only the busy beetle
    Tap-tapping in the wall,

Only from the forest
    The screech-owl's call,
Only the cricket whistling
    While the dew drops fall,
So I know not who came knocking,
At all, at all, at all.

—Walter de la Mare

In the Hall of the Mountain King

from *Peer Gynt Suite*

by *Edvard Grieg*

What makes this music sound spooky?

Halloween

Words and Music by Lynn Freeman Olson

You should know it's the time of year When the gob-lins and ghosts ap - pear. They come at night when there's no more light; Hal-low - een is al - most here. If you look ver-y care-ful - ly, There's a gob-lin be-hind that tree. But I must say, don't you run a-way, 'Cause it might be me!

How would you choose a pumpkin to take home?

Words and Music by Naomi Caldwell

Pick a pick a pump - kin from the pile.

We can make his eyes and a great big smile.

Pick a pick a pump - kin round and clean,

Then we'll be read - y for Hal - low - een!

Hal - low - een, Hal - low - een,

Then we'll be read - y for Hal - low - een!

Turkey Time

Thanksgiving

Thank You
  for all my hands can hold—
    apples red,
      and melons gold,
        yellow corn
          both ripe and sweet,
            peas and beans
              so good to eat!

Thank You
  for all my eyes can see—
    lovely sunlight,
      field and tree,
        white cloud-boats
          in a sea-deep sky,
            soaring bird
              and butterfly.

Thank You
  for all my ears can hear—
    birds' song echoing
      far and near,
        songs of little
          stream, big sea,
            cricket, bullfrog,
              duck and bee!
              —*Ivy O. Eastwick*

Almost every country celebrates the
end of the growing season.

A Turkey Named Bert

Words and Music by Randy DeLelles

With a Swing

A tur-key named Bert thought he'd make up a dance __ and he'd

dance it for the King and Queen. If he did a good job __ and they

liked it a lot __ they would-n't eat him __ that would be mean!

He went side, close, side, close, flap your wings __ and

touch your toes, __ a-gain side, close, side, close,

shake your tail __ and wig-gle your nose. __

LISTENING

Turkey in the Straw

American Folk Song

Square dancing is a kind of American folk
dancing. The music is usually played on a fiddle.
People clap their hands to keep the steady beat. One
person stands aside and calls out the dance steps.
This kind of dancing was very popular with the early
European settlers, and it's still popular today.

OVER THE RIVER AND THROUGH THE WOOD

American Folk Melody
Words by Lydia Maria Childs

1. O - ver the riv - er and through the wood,
2. O - ver the riv - er and through the wood,

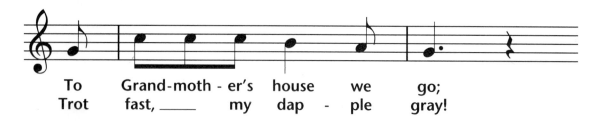

To Grand-moth - er's house we go;
Trot fast, ___ my dap - ple gray!

The horse knows the way to car - ry the sleigh
Spring o - ver the ground like a hunt - ing hound, ___

264 Turkey Time

Through the white and drift - ed snow. _____
_ For this is Thanks-giv - ing day! _____

O - ver the riv - er and through the wood,
O - ver the riv - er and through the wood,

Oh, how the wind does blow!
Now Grand-moth-er's face I spy!

It stings the toes and bites the nose
Hur - rah for the fun! Is the pud - ding done?

As o - ver the ground we go.
Hur - rah for the pump - kin pie!

Winter in the Land of Snow

LISTENING

The Sleigh Ride
from _Musical Sleigh Ride_
by Leopold Mozart

Imagine gliding across a snowy field in a sleigh pulled by trotting horses. What sounds in the music remind you of a sleigh ride?

Jingle Bells

Words and Music by James Pierpont

Verse

Dash-ing through the snow, In a one-horse o-pen sleigh,

O'er the fields we go, Laugh-ing all the way;

Bells on bob-tail ring, Mak-ing spir-its bright,

What fun it is to ride and sing a sleigh-ing song to-night!

Refrain

Jin-gle bells, jin-gle bells, jin-gle all the way!

Oh, what fun it is to ride in a

1. one-horse o-pen sleigh! ___

2. one-horse o-pen sleigh!

Come Light the Candles

Hanukkah is a joyful holiday of lights.

LISTEN to find out how many days Hanukkah lasts.

In the Window

Slowly

Hebrew Folk Song
English Words by Judith Eisenstein

In the win - dow where you can see the glow

Of my me - no - rah on new - ly fall - en snow,

1. I will set you, one lit - tle can - dle,
2. I will set you, two* lit - tle can - dles,

On this the first night of Ha - nuk - kah.
On this the sec-ond* night of Ha - nuk - kah.

* On each of the nights of Hanukkah, sing the correct number.
   On the eighth verse, sing the word "last."

LISTEN for "banish" and "vanish" in this song. What do you think they mean?

Feast of Light

Jewish Folk Melody
Words by Sarah Levi

We have come to ban-ish night, Ban-ish it with can-dle-light.

All the lit-tle can-dle rays Join to make a might-y blaze.

Van-ish dark-ness, van-ish night. Ha-nuk-kah is the feast of light.

Van-ish dark-ness, van-ish night. Ha-nuk-kah is the feast of light.

A VERY BRITISH CHRISTMAS

Americans share many British customs. Some traditions are special to only one place. In a village in England, men hold reindeer antlers over their heads for a holiday dance.

Abbots Bromley Horn Dance

LISTENING

English Folk Music

The Abbots Bromley Horn Dance is a very old dance. No one knows for sure how it started. It is danced each year at Christmas and other holidays. You will hear music played on a recorder.

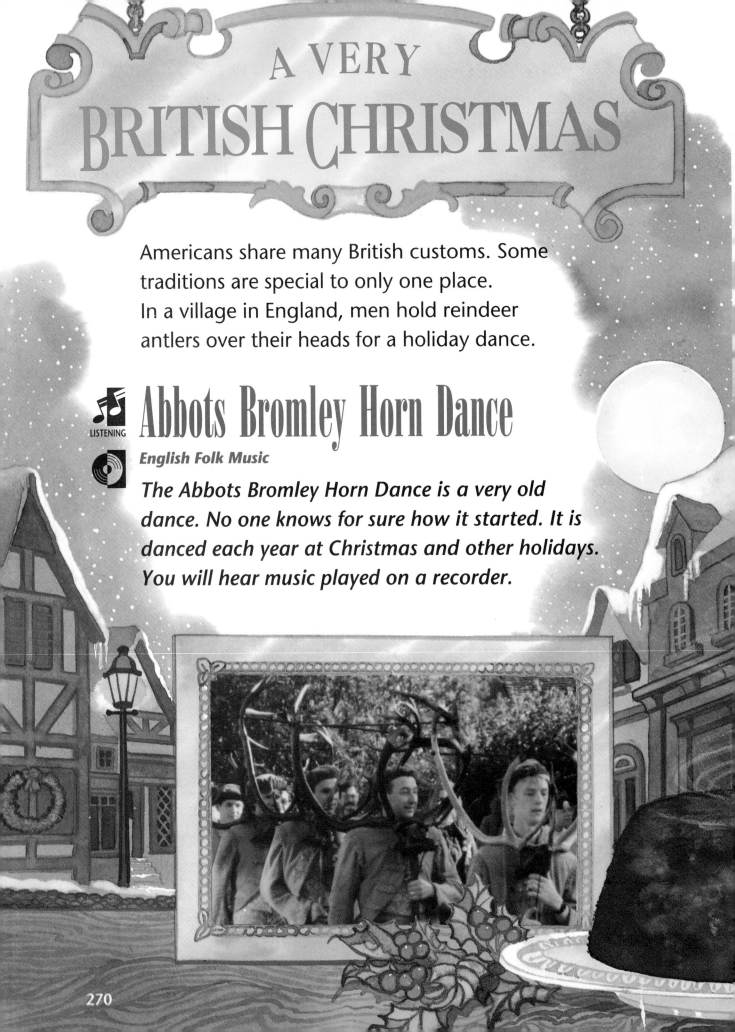

Hundreds of years ago, people in England ate pudding at the beginning of their meal. Now it is a dessert for Christmas dinner.

We Wish You a Merry Christmas

English Carol

1. We wish you a mer - ry Christ - mas,
2. Now bring us some fig - gy pud - ding,
3. For we love our fig - gy pud - ding,
4. We won't go un - til we get some,
5. We wish you a mer - ry Christ - mas,

We wish you a mer - ry Christ - mas,
Now bring us some fig - gy pud - ding,
For we love our fig - gy pud - ding,
We won't go un - til we get some,
We wish you a mer - ry Christ - mas,

We wish you a mer - ry Christ - mas,
Now bring us some fig - gy pud - ding,
For we love our fig - gy pud - ding,
We won't go un - til we get some,
We wish you a mer - ry Christ - mas,

And a hap - py New Year.
And _____ bring it out here.
So _____ bring some out here.
So _____ bring some out here.
And a hap - py New Year.

This English carol tells the story of an imaginary boat trip.

I Saw Three Ships

English Carol

1. I saw three ships come sail - ing in,
2. And what was in those ships all three,
3. 'Twas Jo - seph and his fair la - dy,
4. Then all the bells on earth shall ring,

On Christ-mas Day, on Christ-mas Day;

I saw three ships come sail - ing in,
And what was in those ships all three,
'Twas Jo - seph and his fair la - dy,
Then all the bells on earth shall ring,

On Christ - mas Day in the morn - ing.

What does each animal in the song
do on Christmas?

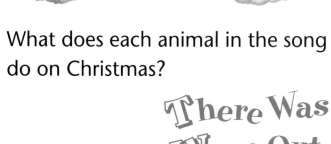

There Was a Pig
Went Out to Dig

English Carol

1. There   was   a   Pig   went   out   to   dig,
2. There   was   a   Cow   went   out   to   plough,
3. There   was   a   Spar-row went   out   to   har-row,

Chris - i - mas   Day,   Chris - i - mas   Day.

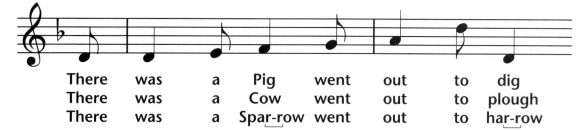

There   was   a   Pig   went   out   to   dig
There   was   a   Cow   went   out   to   plough
There   was   a   Spar-row   went   out   to   har-row

On   Chris - i - mas   Day   in   the   morn - ing!

4. There was a Crow went out to
      sow,
   Chrisimas Day, Chrisimas Day.
   There was a Crow went out to
      sow
   On Chrisimas Day in the morning!

5. There was a Sheep went out to
      reap,
   Chrisimas Day, Chrisimas Day.
   There was a Sheep went out to
      reap
   On Chrisimas Day in the morning!

6. There was a Drake went out to
      rake,
   Chrisimas Day, Chrisimas Day.
   There was a Drake went out to
      rake
   On Chrisimas Day in the morning!

7. There was a Minnow went out to
      winnow,
   Chrisimas Day, Chrisimas Day.
   There was a Minnow went out to
      winnow
   On Chrisimas Day in the morning!

Some African American spirituals are fun to sing because of their rhythm and melody.

GO TELL IT ON THE MOUNTAIN

African American Spiritual

Go, tell it on the moun - tain,

O - ver ___ the hills and ev' - ry - where.

Go, tell it on the moun - tain,

That Je - sus Christ ___ is born.

This carol comes from a part of Spain where the language is a mixture of French and Spanish.

El Noi de la Mare
The Son of Mary

Catalonian Carol
English Version by MMH

Catalan: Què li da-rem a n'el Noi de la Ma-re?
English: What shall we give to the in-fant of Mar-y?

Què li da-rem que li sà-pi-ga bon? Li da-rem pan-ses en
What can we give for the child to en-joy? We shall bring bas-kets of

u-nes ba-lan-ces, Li da-rem fi-gues en un pa-ne-ró.
figs and of rai-sins, These are the gifts for the new ba-by boy.

Li da-rem pan-ses en u-nes ba-lan-ces,
We shall bring bas-kets of figs and of rai-sins,

Li da-rem fi-gues en un pa-ne-ró.
These are the gifts for the new ba-by boy.

Some Jamaicans dance to this song during Christmas parties. It means "Christmas is coming, I want my presents, Christmas is coming, I want my dinner."

CHRISMUS A COME

Jamaican Folk Song

Chris - mus a come me wan' ___ me la - ma.

Chris - mus a come me wan' ___ me la - ma.

Chris - mus a come me wan' ___ me deg - ge - day.

Chris - mus a come me wan' ___ me deg - ge - day.

Evergreen trees are often used for Christmas trees. Why is the word *evergreen* a good name for this tree?

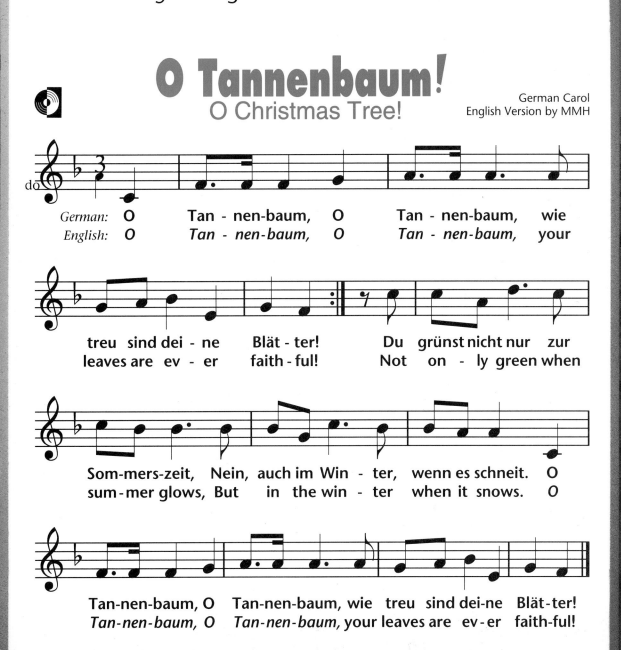

O Tannenbaum!
O Christmas Tree!

German Carol
English Version by MMH

German: O Tan - nen-baum, O Tan - nen-baum, wie
English: O Tan - nen-baum, O Tan - nen-baum, your

treu sind dei - ne Blät - ter! Du grünst nicht nur zur
leaves are ev - er faith-ful! Not on - ly green when

Som-mers-zeit, Nein, auch im Win - ter, wenn es schneit. O
sum-mer glows, But in the win - ter when it snows. O

Tan-nen-baum, O Tan-nen-baum, wie treu sind dei-ne Blät-ter!
Tan-nen-baum, O Tan-nen-baum, your leaves are ev-er faith-ful!

老頭子要買新氈帽老婆子要吃大花糕

THE CHINESE NEW YEAR

New Year is an important holiday for Chinese people everywhere. It is a time for visiting family and friends. It is a time for giving gifts. There are many special foods to eat. The celebration lasts about two weeks. It starts in late January or early February.

You'll find whenever the New Year comes
The Kitchen God will want some plums.
The girls will want some flowers new;
The boys will want firecrackers, too.
A new felt cap will please papa,
And a sugar cake for dear mama.

—*Chinese Mother Goose Rhyme*

新年來到糖瓜祭灶姑娘要花子要炮

恭賀新禧

Dragon Dance *Asian Folk Music*

LISTENING

Lion and Dragon Dances are an exciting part of Chinese New Year. The Lion Dance only needs two people to dance. The Dragon is so big, it needs many people. They have to move together as the dragon.

The Year-Naming Race *Chinese Folk Tale*

Each year of the Chinese calendar is named for an animal. Listen to a story that tells how the years got their names.

Anne Drake, Age 8

Chinese New Year is a long holiday! It ends with the Lantern Festival on the first full moon of the New Year.

GO A TIN

LANTERN SONG

Taiwanese Folk Song
English Version by MMH

Taiwanese: 古　仔　燈　　　古　仔　燈
English: Lan - tern　bright,　　lan - tern　bright,

大　家　來　提　　古　仔　燈
Light　the ___ way,　my ___　lan - tern　bright.

TO CELEBRATE FREEDOM

Martin Luther King, Jr., was a great leader. He
fought for the freedom of African Americans
and people everywhere.

Martin Luther King

Words and Music by Theresa Fulbright

1. He want - ed   peace   and love all   o-ver this   land,
2. He walked for   you   and me all   o-ver this   land,

He want - ed   peace   and love all   o-ver this   land.
He walked for   you   and me all   o-ver this   land.

Mar - tin   Lu - ther King   was   a   peace - lov - ing man,
Mar - tin   Lu - ther King   was   a   great, great ___ man,

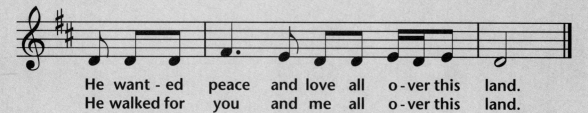

He want - ed   peace   and love all   o - ver this   land.
He walked for   you   and me all   o - ver this   land.

3. He died for freedom's cause to save this land,
   He died for freedom's cause to save this land.
   Martin Luther King was a brave, brave man,
   He died for freedom's cause to save this land.

In Memory

It took a wise man to dream big,
To dream great,
To talk of peace, brotherhood, and love
When all around was hate.
It took a strong man
To stand tall,
To speak of liberty and justice
And dignity for all.
He saw a great country
With some growing still to do.
He dreamed of a better world
Where freedom could ring true.
And so today we'll gather
For a birthday celebration
For a man who sought to change the mind
And heart of a nation.
Of liberty and brotherhood and peace
Today we'll sing
As we celebrate the memory of
Martin Luther King.

— *Ericka Northrop*

Somebody Likes You

Valentine cards are about 200 years old. The first Valentines were decorated with ribbons and lace, and even feathers. What kind of valentines do you like to send?

Love Somebody

American Folk Song

1. Love some-bod-y, yes I do, Love some-bod-y, yes I do,
2. Love some-bod-y, can't guess who, Love some-bod-y, can't guess who,

Love some-bod-y, yes I do, Love some-bod-y but I won't tell who.
Love some-bod-y, can't guess who, Love some-bod-y but I won't tell who.

Love some-bod-y, yes I do, Love some-bod-y, yes I do,

Love some-bod-y, yes I do, And I hope some-bod-y loves me too.

Border Art, Ying Drake, Age 8

284

You Are My Sunshine

Words and Music by Jimmie Davis and Charles Mitchell

You are my sun-shine, _____ my on-ly sun-shine. _____

You make me hap-py _____ when skies are gray. _____

You'll nev-er know, Dear, _____ how much I love you, _____

Please don't take my sun-shine a-way. _____

Most of the words in this song don't really mean anything, but they are still fun to sing!

Skinnamarink

Tin Pan Alley Song

Skin-na-ma-rink a-dink a-dink, skin-na-ma-rink a-doo,

I love you; Skin-na-ma-rink a-dink a-dink,

skin-na-ma-rink a-doo, Yes, I do.

I love you in the morn-ing and in the af-ter-noon,

I love you in the eve-ning, 'neath the sil-v'ry moon.

Skin-na-ma-rink a-dink a-dink, skin-na-ma-rink a-doo,

I love you.

When You Send a Valentine

Words and Music by Mildred J. Hill and Louella Garrett

When you send a Val-en-tine, That's the time for fun.

Push it un - der - neath the door, Ring the bell and

run, run, run, run. Ring the bell and run.

Shamrocks for Luck

Try reading this poem very softly. Think of some other ways you can read it.

The Wearing of the Green

It ought to come in April,
or, better yet, in May
when everything is green as green—
I mean St. Patrick's Day.

With still a week of winter
this wearing of the green
seems rather out of season—
it's rushing things, I mean.

But maybe March *is* better
when all is done and said:
St. Patrick brings a promise,
a four-leaf-clover promise,
a green-all-over promise
of springtime just ahead!

—Aileen Fisher

LISTENING

Tune for Mairéad and Anna Ní Mhaonaigh *by Dáithí Sproule*

"Tune for Mairéad and Anna Ní Mhaonaigh" was written by guitarist Dáithí Sproule when he went to the birthday party for these two girls. He felt bad because he didn't have a gift for them. Before the evening was over, he composed this tune as a present.

ROBINS AND RAINBOWS

It's spring!
Listen and look for signs
of spring in this song.

SPRINGTIME

Words and Music by Lynn Freeman Olson

Spring-time! I can tell that it's here; Spring-time! Ev'-ry
sign's ver-y clear: Sun-shine and show-ers
Bloom-ing the flow-ers. Spring-time! Take a
ride on a swing; Spring-time! Get a kite on a string.
Fare-well to Win-ter; I'm glad it's Spring!

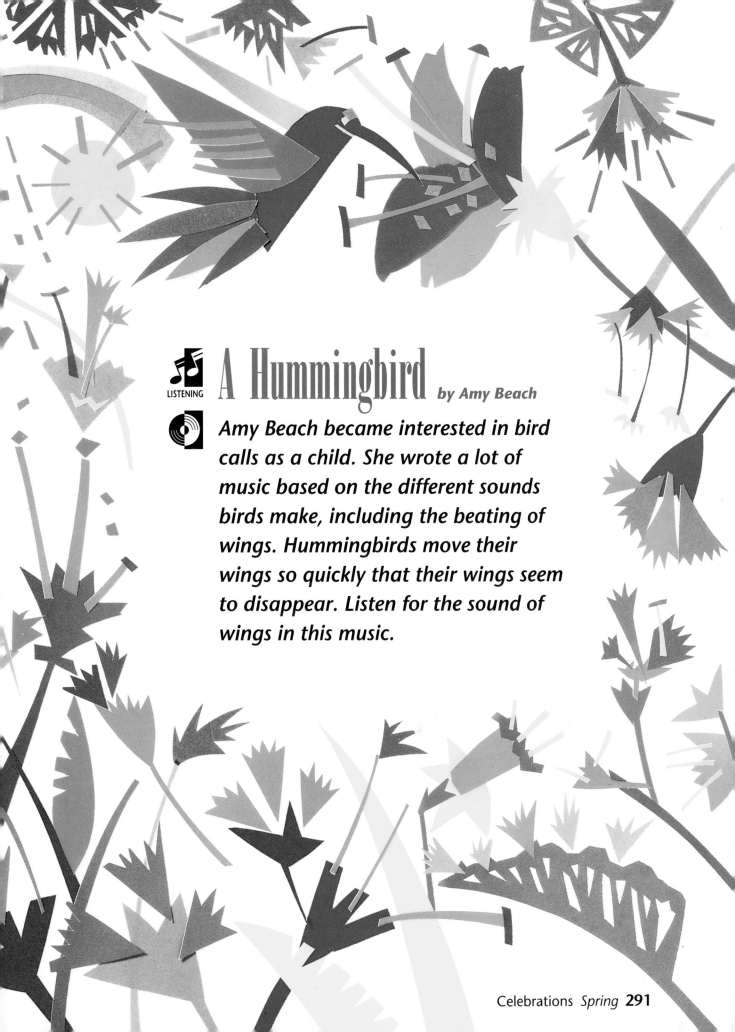

A Hummingbird by *Amy Beach*

LISTENING

Amy Beach became interested in bird calls as a child. She wrote a lot of music based on the different sounds birds make, including the beating of wings. Hummingbirds move their wings so quickly that their wings seem to disappear. Listen for the sound of wings in this music.

Many birds migrate north in the spring. You may see different kinds of birds than you saw in winter.

THERE CAME TO MY WINDOW

English Folk Song

do

There came to my win-dow one morn-ing in spring,

A sweet lit - tle rob - in, he came there to sing.

The song that he sang, it was pret-ti-er by far,

Than __ an - y I heard on a flute or gui - tar.

Everything seems fresh and new in spring.

SPOTLIGHT ON **LOUIS ARMSTRONG**

Louis Armstrong was a great trumpet player. He was also known for his rough, throaty singing voice. Can you imagine what the word *throaty* means? As you listen to him sing, try to find other words to tell how his voice sounds.

♪ LISTENING

💿 **What a Wonderful World**
by George Weiss and Bob Thiele, sung by Louis Armstrong

Photo by Philippe Halsman © Yvonne Halsman

In India, there is a spring celebration called *Holi*. It is known as the Color Festival in English. It's time for the festival when colors come back to the trees, grass, and flowers.

People squirt each other with colored water and throw colored powder.

LISTENING

Holi Song
collected by Kathy B. Sorensen

as sung by Chhanda Chakroborti

Listen as the singer's voice slides from note to note.

Lemonade

American Singing Game

Group 1 | Group 2

Here we come! (Where from?)

Group 1 | Group 2

New York. (What's your trade?)

Group 1 | Group 2

Lem - on - ade. (Give us some!)

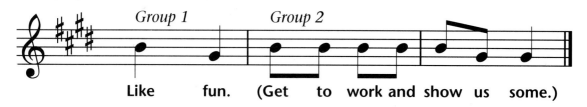

Group 1 | Group 2

Like fun. (Get to work and show us some.)

Snail, Snail

American Singing Game

Snail, snail, snail, snail,

'Round and 'round and 'round and 'round.

We Are Playing in the Forest

American Singing Game

We are play - ing in the for - est

for the wolf is far a - way.

Who knows what will hap - pen to us

if he finds us at our play?

Bluebells

American Jump Rope Song

Blue-bells, cock-le shells, ee - vy, i - vy o - ver-head.

My moth - er said that I was born in

Jan - u - ar - y, Feb - ru - ar - y, March, Ap - ril,

May, June, Ju - ly, Au - gust,

Sep - tem - ber, Oc - to - ber, No - vem - ber, De - cem - ber.

2468

Two, Four, Six, Eight

English Nursery Rhyme
Music by Marilyn Davidson

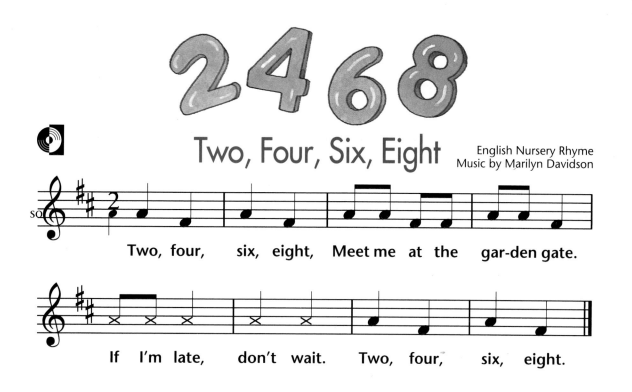

Two, four, six, eight, Meet me at the gar-den gate.

If I'm late, don't wait. Two, four, six, eight.

Mr. Frog

American Singing Game

On a log, Mis - ter Frog

Sang a song the whole day long,

Glumph, Glumph, Glumph.

English Folk Song

Hot cross buns, Hot cross buns,

One a pen-ny, two a pen-ny, Hot cross buns.

Cambodian Singing Game
Collected and Transcribed by Kathy B. Sorensen

Cambodian: លាក់ ក ខ្សៀង ឆ្មា ខាំ កែង អោស លោង អោស លោង

English: Hide the towel, catch the cat, me - ow, me - ow.

Nabe, Nabe, Soku, Nuke

Stewpot, Stewpot, Bottomless Pot

Japanese Singing Game
English Version by MMH

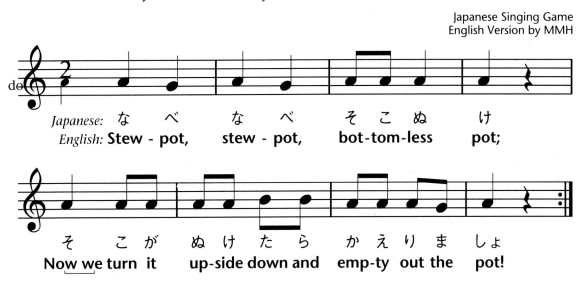

Japanese: な べ な べ そ こ ぬ け
English: Stew - pot, stew - pot, bot-tom-less pot;

そ こ が ぬ け た ら か え り ま しょ
Now we turn it up-side down and emp-ty out the pot!

Shoheen Sho

Welsh Folk Song
Verse 1 Traditional Welsh Words
Verses 2 and 3 by Margaret Campbelle-duGard

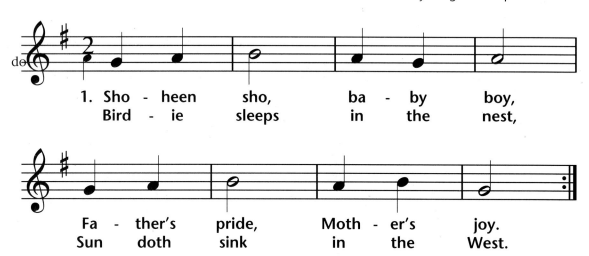

1. Sho - heen sho, ba - by boy,
Bird - ie sleeps in the nest,

Fa - ther's pride, Moth - er's joy.
Sun doth sink in the West.

2. Shoheen sho, baby girl,
   Father's pride, Mother's pearl.
   Birdie sleeps in the nest,
   Sun doth sink in the West.

3. Shoheen sho, little dove,
   Fill my heart full of love.
   Birdie sleeps in the nest,
   Sun doth sink in the West.

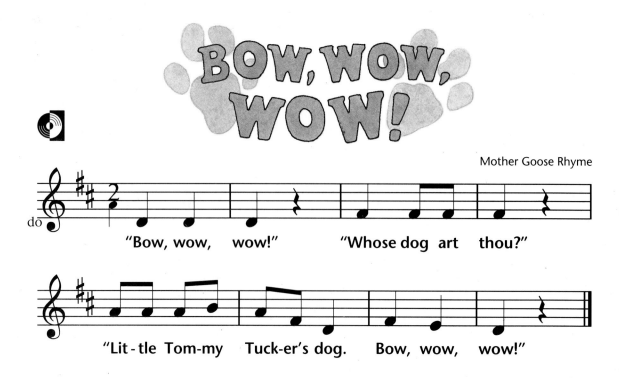

Mother Goose Rhyme

"Bow, wow, wow!" "Whose dog art thou?"

"Lit - tle Tom-my Tuck-er's dog. Bow, wow, wow!"

Pizza, Pizza, Daddy-O

African American Singing Game

An-nie has a boy-friend, Piz - za, piz - za, dad-dy - o,

How do you know it? Piz - za, piz - za, dad-dy - o,

'Cause she told me, Piz - za, piz - za, dad-dy - o,

Let's rope it! Rope it, rope __ it, dad-dy - o,
Let's swim it! Swim it, swim __ it, dad-dy - o,
Let's duck it! Duck it, duck __ it, dad-dy - o,

Let's twist it! Twist it, twist __ it, dad-dy - o,

Let's end it, end it, end __ it, dad-dy - o!

LENNY

Words and Music by Minnie O'Leary

1. Len - ny, Len - ny has so _____ man - y
2. Jen - ny, Jen - ny can be _____ an - y -
3. Here's a pen - ny, Len - ny, _____ Len - ny,

dreams in his clev - er head. _____
thing that she dreams to be. _____
dressed ___ in den - im blue. _____

Build - ing cas - tles, hang - ing stars on
Danc - er, bak - er, mus - ic - mak - er,
Make a wish just like my wish that

shin - ing gold - en thread, _____ on
sail - or on the sea, _____ or
all your dreams come true, _____ that

shin - ing gold - en thread. _____
sail - or on the sea. _____
all your dreams come true. _____

All come true. _____

BUENOS DÍAS, AMIGO

Good Day, Friend

Latin American Folk Song
English Version by MMH

Spanish: **Bue-nos dí-as, a - mi-go,**   **¿có-mo es-tás hoy**   **dí - a?**
English: ***Bue-nos dí-as, a - mi-go;***   **how are you this**   **morn-ing?**

¿Quie - res a-pren-der un jue - go?   **Yo te lo voy a en-se - ñar.**
Would you like to learn a new game? I will teach it to you now.

American Folk Song

Old King Glo - ry of the moun - tain,

The moun - tain reached so high,

It near - ly reached the sky.

The first one, the sec - ond one,

the third fol - low me.

Qué bonito es
HOW WONDERFUL IT IS

Words and Music by Belle San Miguel-Ortiz
English Version by MMH

Spanish: O - ye, o - ye, _____ qué bo - ni - to es.
English: O - ye, o - ye, ___ how won-der-ful it is.

Can - to, le - o _____ dos idio-mas bi - en.
Sing - ing, read - ing, two lan-gua-ges so well.

Dí - gan-me to - dos, _____ yo tri - un - fa - ré, _____
Eve - ry-one tells me, this is the best of all: _____

Al ser bi - lin - güe _____ qué bo - ni - to es. _____
To be bi - lin - gual, how won-der-ful it is! _____

Al ser bi - lin - güe _____ qué bo - ni - to es.
To be bi - lin - gual, how won-der-ful it is!

Good Friends

Words and Music by Carol Huffman

Good friends al - ways stick to - geth - er;

That's what a friend is al - ways for.

Good friends al - ways stick to - geth - er,

Be - ing friends for - ev - er more.

Ghanaian Folk Song
Collected by Mona Lowe

Leader

Fanti: **Tu - e Tu - e   ba - ri - ma   tu - e tu - e**

Group

(Tu - e Tu - e   ba - ri - ma   tu - e tu - e)

Leader

A - bo - fra   ba   A - ma da - wa da - wa   tu - e tu - e

Group

(A - bo - fra   ba   A - ma da - wa da - wa   tu - e tu - e)

All

Hei - ba - ri - ma   tu - e tu - e Hei - ba - ri - ma

German Folk Song

The more we get to - geth-er, to - geth-er, to - geth-er,

The more we get to - geth - er, the hap-pier we'll be!

For your friends are my friends, and my friends are your friends,

The more we get to - geth - er, the hap-pier we'll be!

310

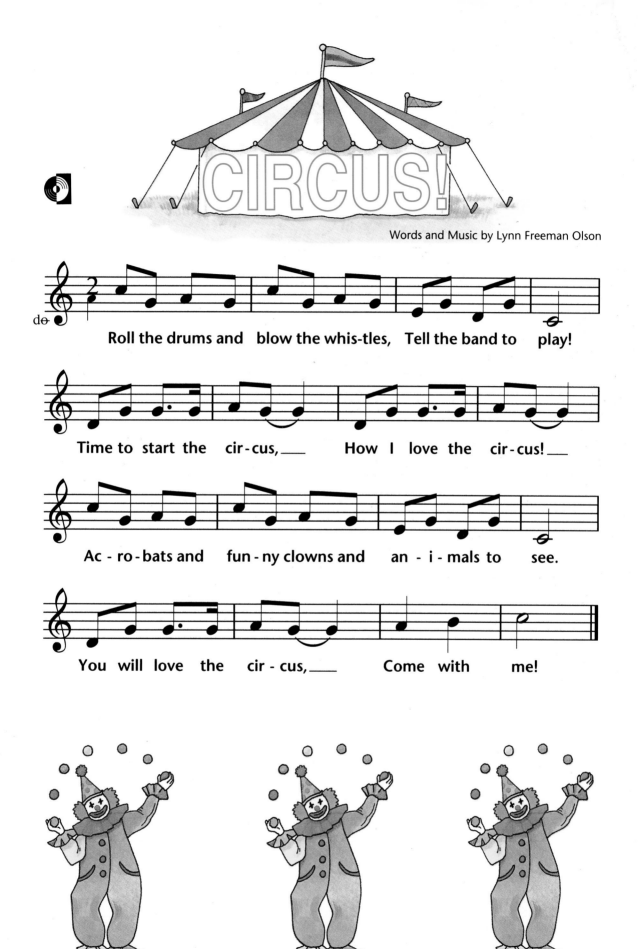

Words and Music by Lynn Freeman Olson

Roll the drums and blow the whis-tles, Tell the band to play!

Time to start the cir-cus, ___ How I love the cir-cus! ___

Ac-ro-bats and fun-ny clowns and an-i-mals to see.

You will love the cir-cus, ___ Come with me!

Sieben Steps

Seven Steps

German Folk Song

German: **Eins, zwei, drei, vier,   fünf, sechs, sieben,   Eins, zwei, drei, vier,**

fünf, sechs, sieben,   Eins, zwei, drei,   eins, zwei, drei,

Eins, zwei, drei, eins, zwei, drei, Eins, zwei, drei, vier, fünf, sechs, sieben.

Russian Folk Melody
Words by Cecil Cowdrey

1. **When the snow is   fly - ing,   Hear the North Wind cry - ing!**
2. **When the rain-drops pat - ter,   Lis - ten how   they chat - ter!**

Ooh, __ hear it blow!   Ooh, __ see it snow!
Ooh, __ how they splash,   On my win - dow sash!

312

VAMOS A LA MAR

LET'S GO TO THE SEA

Guatemalan Folk Song
English Version by MMH

Spanish: Va - mos a la mar, tum tum,
English: Let's go to the sea, tum tum,

a co - mer pes - ca - do, tum tum;
We will eat some fish - es, tum tum;

bo - ca co - lo - ra - da, tum tum,
Bo - ca co - lo - ra - da, tum tum,

fri - ti - to y a - sa - do, tum tum.
Fried and hot and spi - cy, tum tum.

Ev'ry Time I'm Feeling BLUE

Words and Music by Margaret Campbelle-duGard

1.–4. Ev'-ry time I'm feel-ing blue,

1.
(1.) I clap my hands like this.
(2.) I snap my fin-gers like this.
(3.) I nod my head like this.
(4.) I move my feet like this.

2.
clap my hands like this.
snap my fin-gers like this.
nod my head like this.
move my feet like this.

Like this, like this,

like this, like this.

Going over the Sea

Canadian Street Rhyme

Verse

1. When I was one I ate a bun,
2. When I was two I buck-led my shoe,
3. When I was three I banged my knee, Go-ing o-ver the sea.
4. When I was four I shut the door,
5. When I was five I learned to jive,

I jumped a-board a sail-or-man's ship, And the sail-or-man said to

Refrain

me, "Go - ing o - ver, go - ing un - der, Stand at at -

ten - tion like a sol - dier, With a one, two, and three."

6. When I was six I picked up sticks, . . .

7. When I was seven I went to heaven, . . .

8. When I was eight I learned to skate, . . .

9. When I was nine I climbed a vine, . . .

10. When I was ten I caught a hen, . . .

Music by Carole King
Words by Maurice Sendak

1. In January it's so nice, while slipping on the sliding ice,
   To sip hot chicken soup with rice.
   Sipping once, sipping twice, sipping chicken soup
   with rice.

2. In February it will be my snowman's anniversary,
   With cake for him and soup for me!
   Happy once, happy twice, happy chicken soup with rice.

3. In March the wind blows down the door and spills my
   soup upon the floor.
   It laps it up and roars for more.
   Blowing once, blowing twice, blowing chicken soup
   with rice.

4. In April I will go away, to far-off Spain or old Bombay,
   And dream about hot soup all day.
   Oh my once, oh my twice, oh my chicken soup with rice.

5. In May I truly think it best to be a robin lightly dressed,
   Concocting soup inside my nest.
   Mix it once, mix it twice, mix that chicken soup with rice.

6. In June I saw a charming group of roses all begin to droop.
   I pepped them up with chicken soup!
   Sprinkle once, sprinkle twice, sprinkle chicken soup
   with rice.

7. In July I'll take a peep into the cool and fishy deep,
   Where chicken soup is selling cheap,
   Selling once, selling twice, selling chicken soup
   with rice.

8. In August it will be so hot, I will become a cooking pot,
   Cooking soup of course. Why not?
   Cooking once, cooking twice, cooking chicken soup
   with rice.

9. In September for a while, I will ride a crocodile
   Down the chicken soupy Nile.
   Paddle once, paddle twice, paddle chicken soup
   with rice.

10. In October I'll be host to witches, goblins and a ghost.
    I'll serve them chicken soup on toast.
    Whoopy once, whoopy twice, whoopy chicken soup
    with rice.

11. In November's gusty gale I will flop my flippy tail
    And spout hot soup. I'll be a whale!
    Spouting once, spouting twice, spouting chicken soup
    with rice.

12. In December I will be a baubled, bangled Christmas tree
    With soup bowls draped all over me.
    Merry once, merry twice, merry chicken soup with rice.

All 'Round the Brickyard

Play Party Game Adapted from
African American Folk Song

All 'round the brick-yard, re-mem-ber me. I'm goin' to

step it, step it, step it and-a re-mem-ber me.

Hey, Mr. Monday

Words and Music by Barbara Andress
Adapted by Sue Snyder

1. Hey, Mis - ter Mon - day,
2. Hey, Miss ___ Tues - day,
3. Hey, Doc - tor Wednes-day, } Play a song, play a song,
4. Hey, Se - ñor Thurs - day,
5. Hey, Se-ño-ri-ta Fri - day,

Hey, Mis - ter Mon - day,
Hey, Miss ___ Tues - day,
Hey, Doc - tor Wednes-day, } Play a song for me.
Hey, Se - ñor Thurs - day,
Hey, Se-ño-ri-ta Fri - day,

6. Hey, Mrs. Saturday . . .   7. Hey, Captain Sunday . . .

318

Clickety Clack

Words and Music by Hap Palmer and Martha Cheney

A *Solo*

1.–4. Car - ry - ing { lum - ber / coal ___ / pro - duce / grain ___ } down the track; ___

Go to B *after verses 2 and 4.*

Go - ing to the cit - y and it won't come ___ back.

B *All*

Woo, woo, click-e-ty clack, This old train ___ is ___ load-ed down. ___ Woo, woo, click-e-ty clack, This old train ___ is ___ cit-y bound. ___

Dinosaur Tooth Care

Words and Music by
Barbara Mariconda and Denise Puccio

Verse

1. Well, I went to the di-no-saur den-tist To
2. I went back to the di-no-saur val-ley; I

clean my di-no-saur teeth. He flossed and brushed and
brushed both morn-ing and night. The di - no clan all

swished and flushed all a-round and un - der-neath. "Say,
gath - ered 'round just to see my pearl - y whites. And

Doc, now I want you to tell me How to
then they all asked me to teach 'em How to

keep these chop-pers clean." "Well, I'll tell you, son, it
floss and brush just right. Now our teeth are all so

can be done, And this is what __ I mean:
white and bright, Our smiles are di - no - mite!

Refrain *(repeat for each verse)*

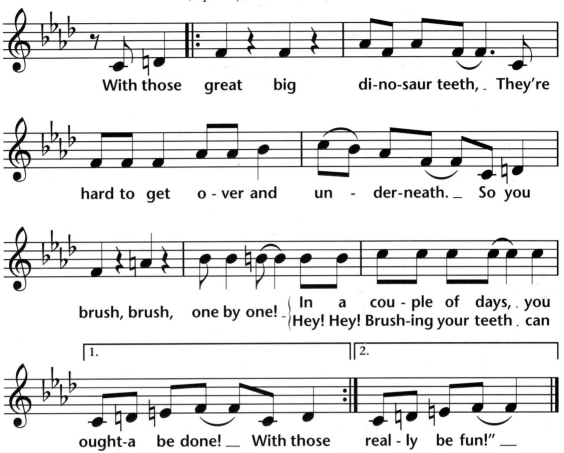

With those   great   big   di-no-saur teeth,__ They're

hard to get   o - ver and   un - der-neath. __ So you

brush, brush,   one by one! { In   a   cou - ple of days, __ you
Hey! Hey! Brush-ing your teeth __ can

1.
ought-a   be done! __ With those

2.
real - ly   be fun!" __

"Dinosaur Tooth Care" from *More Sounds We Found* by Barbara Mariconda & Denise Puccio. © Copyright MCMLXXXIII Wide World
Music, Inc.

I LIVE IN A CITY

Words and Music by Malvina Reynolds

Refrain

I live in a cit-y, yes, I do, I live in a cit-y, yes, I do,

End (Fine)

I live in a cit-y, yes, I do, __ Made by hu-man hands.

Verse

1. Black hands, white hands, yel-low and brown, All to-geth-er
2. Brown hands, yel-low hands, white __ and black, Mined the coal and
3. Black hands, brown hands, yel-low and white, Built the build-ings
4. Black hands, white hands, brown __ and tan, Milled the flour and

built this town, Black hands, white hands, yel - low and brown,
built the stack, Brown hands, yel-low hands, white ___ and black,
tall and bright, Black hands, brown hands, yel - low and white,
cleaned the pan, Black hands, white hands, brown and tan, The

*Go back to the begining and sing to the End.
(Da Capo al Fine)*

All to - geth - er make the wheels go round.
Built the en - gine and laid the track.
Filled them all ___ with ___ shin - ing light.
work - ing wom-an and the work - ing man.

322

American Folk Song

1. There were ten
2. There were nine
3. There were eight } in a bed and the lit-tle one said,
4. There were sev-en
5. There were six

"Roll o - ver! Roll o - ver!"

So they all rolled o - ver and one fell out!

Last verse only

10. There was one in the bed, and the lit-tle one said, "Good night!"

6. There were five . . .

7. There were four . . .

8. There were three . . .

9. There were two . . .

Old Blue

Southern Mountain Song

1. I had a dog and his name was Blue,
2. Chased that ___ pos-sum up a hol - low tree,
3. Caught that ___ pos-sum up a hol - low tree,
4. Baked that ___ pos - sum ___ good and brown,

I had a dog and his name was Blue,
Chased that ___ pos-sum up a hol - low tree,
Caught that ___ pos-sum up a hol - low tree,
Baked that ___ pos - sum ___ good and brown,

I had a dog and his name was Blue, and I
Chased that ___ pos-sum up a hol - low tree, _____
Caught that ___ pos-sum up a hol - low tree, _____
Baked that ___ pos - sum ___ good and brown, _____

bet - cha five dol - lars he's a good dog, too.
Best ___ hunt-in' dog ___ you ___ ev-er did see.
Best ___ hunt-in' dog ___ you ___ ev-er did see.
Laid ___ sweet po-ta - ters ___ all a - round.

Here, Blue, you good dog, you.

5. Old Blue died, he died one day,
   So I dug his grave and I buried him away.

6. I dug his grave with a silver spade,
   Lowered him down with a golden chain.

7. When I get to heaven there's one thing I'll do,
   I'll grab me a horn and blow for Blue!

Mos', Mos'!
CAT, CAT!

Hopi Singing Game
Collected by David McAllester
English Version by MMH

Hopi: Mos', mos', nai - ti - la, mos', mos', nai - ti - la,
English: Cat, Cat! Cat, he steals! Cat, Cat! Cat, he steals!

Ka - nel per - kye nai - ti - la, Ka - nel per - kye
Sheep-skin, Sheep-skin, Cat, he steals! Sheep-skin, Sheep-skin,

nai - ti - la, Mo - sa! __ Mo - sa! nya, nya, nya
Cat, he steals! Cat! _____ Cat! _____ Meow meow meow

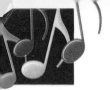

American Folk Song

Down   by the   bay,   where the wa-ter-mel-ons grow,

Back   to   my   home   I   dare not   go,

For if   I   do   my moth-er will   say,

1. "Did you   ev - er see a goose _____ kiss - ing a moose,
2. "Did you   ev - er see a whale with a   pol - ka dot __ tail,
3. "Did you   ev - er see a fly _____ wear - ing a tie,
4. "Did you   ev - er see a bear _____ comb - ing his hair,
5. "Did you   ev - er see __lla-mas _____   eat - ing their pa-ja-mas,
6. "Did you   ev - er have a time when you could-n't make a rhyme,

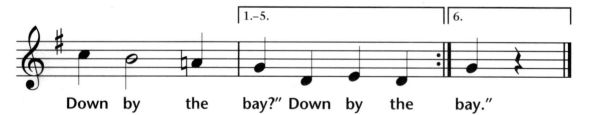

Down by   the   bay?" Down by   the   bay."

326

BRINCA LA TABLITA

Hop on the *Tablita*

Puerto Rican Folk Song
English Version by MMH

Spanish: **Brin-ca la ta - bli-ta, ya yo la brin - qué.**
English: **Hop on the *ta - bli - ta*, I have had my turn.**

Brin-ca la tu a - ho - ra que yo me can - sé.
Hop a-cross, it's your turn now, and I am tired.

Reprinted from *Canciones de Mi Isla,* published by ARTS Inc.,
32 Market Street, New York, NY, 10002, a resource center in
the Chinese and Hispanic cultures on the Lower East Side
since 1970.

Blackie

Music by Kir Kuklowsky
Words by Elizabeth Kuklowsky

Ukrainian: Ось со-ба-ка Жуч-ка, Хвос-тик як кар - люч-ка. Він все
English: **Here is lit-tle Black-ie, with his tail so wa-cky. Black-ie's**

ду - же злий. Сам на масть ря - бий! Гав гав.
teeth are keen, fluf-fy fur is clean! Bow wow!

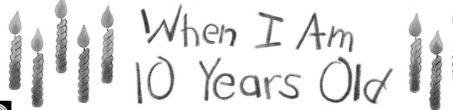

When I Am 10 Years Old

Norwegian Folk Song
Collected by Jane Farwell

1.–11. When I am {1. ten years old, / 2. twen-ty old,} Boom fa-lee-la-lee, Boom fa-lee-lay,

{1. Then I to school must go, / 2. Then I a - court - ing go,} Boom fa - lee - la - lee - lay.

When I am {1. ten years old, / 2. twen - ty old,} Then I to / Then I a -

school must go, / court - ing go,} Boom fa - lee - la - lee, Boom fa - lee-lay,

Boom fa - lee - la - lee - lay, Cho - hay!

3. . . .thirty old, . . .I wear a band
   of gold, . . .

4. . . .forty old, . . .Oh, how my
   family grows, . . .

5. . . .fifty old, . . .My hair is gray
   with gold, . . .

6. . . .sixty old, . . .My hair is white
   as snow, . . .

7. . . .seventy old, . . .I have no hair at all! . . .

8. . . .eighty old, . . .Oh, how the backaches grow, . . .

9. . . .ninety old, . . .Then I to heaven go, . . .

10. . . .hundred old, . . .I wear two wings of gold, . . .

11. . . .thousand old, . . .Oh, how my spirits roam! . . .

Sylvester the Snake

Smoothly, with Lots of Expression

Words and Music by Kay Stephens

Syl - ves - ter the Snake is a sing - ing snake.

He loves to sing in the show - er. Laaaa!

He slith - ers and slides as he lath - ers with soap,

And hiss - es his songs by the hour. ___ Sss - Sss!

SCRATCH ME BACK

Words and Music by Harry Belafonte
and Irving Burgie

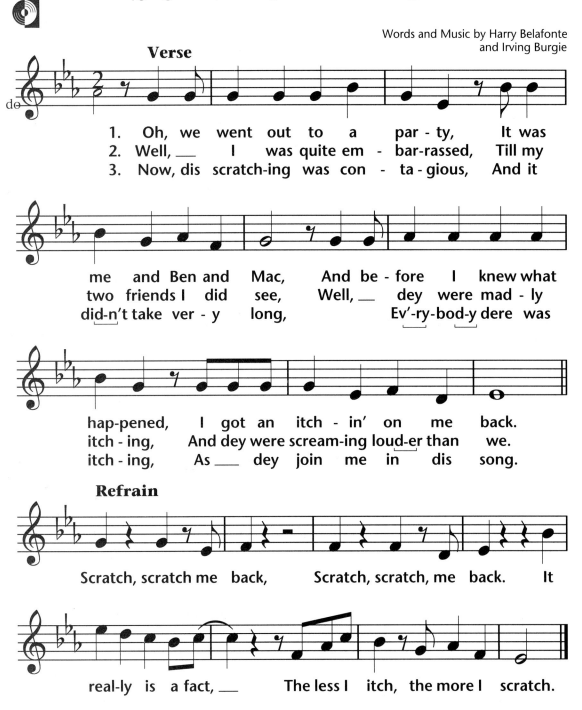

Verse

1. Oh, we went out to a par-ty, It was me and Ben and Mac, And be-fore I knew what hap-pened, I got an itch-in' on me back.
2. Well, ___ I was quite em-bar-rassed, Till my two friends I did see, Well, ___ dey were mad-ly itch-ing, And dey were scream-ing loud-er than we.
3. Now, dis scratch-ing was con-ta-gious, And it did-n't take ver-y long, Ev'-ry-bod-y dere was itch-ing, As ___ dey join me in dis song.

Refrain

Scratch, scratch me back, Scratch, scratch, me back. It real-ly is a fact, ___ The less I itch, the more I scratch.

Tinga Layo

West Indies Calypso Song
English Words by Merrill Staton

Refrain

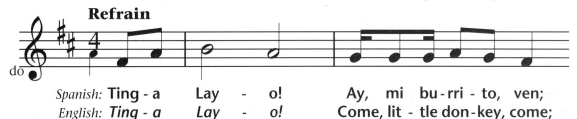

Spanish: **Ting - a Lay - o!** Ay, mi bu - rri - to, ven;
English: *Ting - a Lay - o!* Come, lit - tle don - key, come;

to verse

Ting - a Lay - o! Ay, mi bu - rri - to, ven.
Ting - a Lay - o! Come, lit - tle don - key, come.

— *Last time only* — **Verse**

Ay, mi bu - rri - to, ven. 1. Bu - rri - to
Come, lit - tle don - key, come. 1. My don - key

sí, bu - rri - to no, bu - rri - to co - me con te - ne - dor.
yes, my don-key no, My don-key sit when I say to go.

2. My donkey haw, my donkey gee,
My donkey don't do a thing for me.
Refrain

3. My donkey balk, my donkey bray,
My donkey won't hear a thing I say.
Refrain

1845 Singing School Song

Morn-ing bells I love to hear Ring-ing mer-ri-ly loud and clear.

Words and Music by Mary Ann Hall

Take a bite of mu-sic, __ it real-ly is a treat.

Take a bite of mu-sic, __ serve it with a beat.

Take a bite of mu-sic, __ there are man-y ways __ to play.

Ev'-ry-bod-y needs it ___ ev-er-y day. ___

A la rueda de San Miguel

To the Wheel of St. Michael

Mexican Folk Song
English Version by MMH

Spanish: A la rue - da de San Mi - guel,
English: To the wheel of ___ San Mi - guel,

to - dos tra - en su ca - ja de miel.
Eve - ry - one brings a keg ___ of hon-ey.

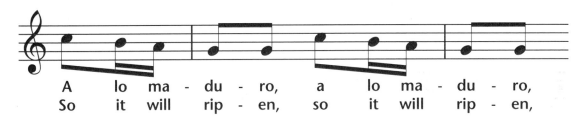

A lo ma - du - ro, a lo ma - du - ro,
So it will rip - en, so it will rip - en,

que se vol - te - e (Pan - cho) de bu - rro.
And keep on turn - ing, (Pan - cho) *de bu - rro.*

Chiapanecas
Ladies of Chiapas

Mexican Folk Song
English Version by MMH

A

Spanish: 1. Cuan-do la no-che lle - gó,
English: 1. Now that the night has ar - rived,

Spanish: 2. El blan-co ran-cho cu - brió,
English: 2. Un - der the moon shin-ing white,

y con su man - to de a - zul
un - der a man - tle of blue,

a - le - gre el bai-le em-pe - zó.
I will go danc-ing with you.

B

Bai - la, mi chia - pa - ne - ca.
Dance, now, my chia - pa - ne - ca.

Bai - la, bai - la con gar - bo.
Dance with grace and en - chant-ment.

(1.) Bai - la, sua - ve ra - yo de
(1.) Dance, now, with the moon ___ shin - ing

(2.) que en el bai - le rei - na e - res
(2.) Dance, my gen - tle one, ___ You will

1.
luz. ___
bright. ___

2.
tú, chia-pa - ne - ca gen - til.
soon be the queen of the dance!

Korean Folk Song
English Version by MMH

Korean: 새 야 새 야 파 랑 새 야
English: **Blue - bird, blue - bird, love - ly blue - bird,**

녹 두 밭 에 앉 지 마 라
Please do not sit in the bean field!

A PARIS
TO PARIS

Cajun Folk Song
English Version by MMH

French: A Pa - ris, à Pa - ris, sur un pe - tit che - val gris.
English: To Pa - ree, to Pa - ree, on a lit - tle horse of gray.

A Guey - dan, à Guey - dan, sur un pe - tit che - val blanc.
To Guey - dan, to Guey - dan, on a lit - tle horse of white.

A Pont Breaux, à Pont Breaux, sur un p'tit ch'val à gal - op.
To Pont Breaux, to Pont Breaux, my lit - tle horse will run a - way.

A SHEPHERD SONG

Israeli Folk Song
Translated by Moshe Jacobson
and Eugene W. Troth

On the plain a shep-herd boy, call-ing for his sheep;
Plays this tune up - on his flute, call-ing them to sleep.

Loo loo loo loo loo loo loo loo loo loo loo.

American Folk Song

Shoo, fly, don't both-er me, Shoo, fly, don't both-er me,

Shoo, fly, don't both-er me, For I be-long to some-bod-y.

I feel, I feel, I feel, I feel like a morn-ing star,

I feel, I feel, I feel, I feel, I feel like a morn-ing star.

Oh, Shoo, fly, don't both-er me, Shoo, fly, don't both-er me,

Shoo, fly, don't both-er me, For I be-long to some-bod-y.

Arabic Folk Song
Words Adapted by Sally Monsour

English: Taf - ta Hin - di, Taf - ta Hin - di, Who will buy some

clothes to __ wear? Silks and sat - ins, love - ly lac - es,

Gold and sil - ver for your hair; Silks and sat - ins,

love - ly lac - es, Gold and sil - ver for your hair.

Arabic: تفتا هندي تفتا هندي شاش أبيع يا بنات
افتحولي يا صبايا ولا خش من الشباك

JENNIE JENKINS

American Folk Song

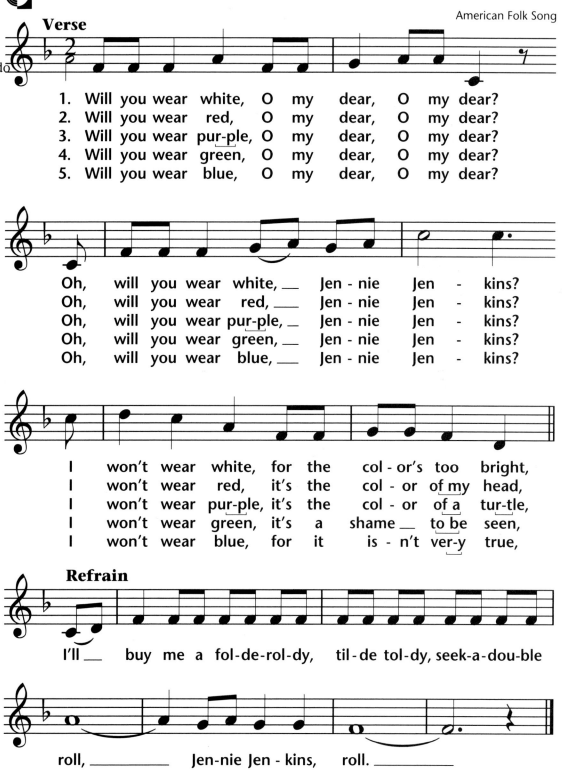

Verse

1. Will you wear white, O my dear, O my dear?
2. Will you wear red, O my dear, O my dear?
3. Will you wear pur-ple, O my dear, O my dear?
4. Will you wear green, O my dear, O my dear?
5. Will you wear blue, O my dear, O my dear?

Oh, will you wear white, __ Jen-nie Jen - kins?
Oh, will you wear red, __ Jen-nie Jen - kins?
Oh, will you wear pur-ple, __ Jen-nie Jen - kins?
Oh, will you wear green, __ Jen-nie Jen - kins?
Oh, will you wear blue, __ Jen-nie Jen - kins?

I won't wear white, for the col-or's too bright,
I won't wear red, it's the col-or of my head,
I won't wear pur-ple, it's the col-or of a tur-tle,
I won't wear green, it's a shame __ to be seen,
I won't wear blue, for it is-n't ver-y true,

Refrain

I'll __ buy me a fol-de-rol-dy, til-de tol-dy, seek-a-dou-ble

roll, _____ Jen-nie Jen - kins, roll. _____

YOU'RE
INVITED:

OUTDOOR
BAND
CONCERT

TICKET

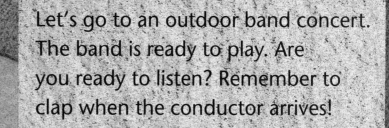

Let's go to an outdoor band concert. The band is ready to play. Are you ready to listen? Remember to clap when the conductor arrives!

🎵 Band Concert
LISTENING
💿 Program

Tattoo No. 1 in F
by Ludwig van Beethoven

The Stars and Stripes Forever
by John Philip Sousa

Entry of the Gladiators
by Julius Fučik

Listening

Listen to more music. Which of these pieces would you like to hear?

Eine Kleine Nachtmusik
Third Movement
WOLFGANG AMADEUS MOZART
1787

Waltz No. 1
KATHARINA
CIBBINI-KOZELUCH
1832

Children's Chorus (excerpt)
from *Carmen*
GEORGES BIZET
1875

Discoveries

The Aquarium
from *The Carnival of the Animals*
CAMILLE SAINT-SAËNS
1886

Children's Symphony
Third Movement
HARL McDONALD
1950

Seventy Six Trombones
from Meredith Willson's *The Music Man*
MEREDITH WILLSON
1957

The Selfish Giant

From a Story by Oscar Wilde
Words and Music by John Horman

Once there was a Selfish Giant who had a large, lovely garden. Children who passed by each day would stop to play among the beautiful trees and flowers that grew there.

How Happy We Are Here

With a Bounce
Children in Garden

Words and Music by John Horman

do

1. How hap - py we are here. _____
2. Come join our fun to - day! _____

How hap - py we are here. _____
For - ev - er let us stay. _____

From morn - ing sun to close of day, ___
A - mong the trees and grass so green. ___

come join us as we sing and play ___
With star - like flow - ers in be - tween. ___

in the gar - den of good cheer! _____
How ___ hap - py we are here! _____

In the gar - den of good cheer!
How ___ hap - py we are here!

The Giant was away, so the children played in his garden without fear. One day he returned and found them there. He was very angry!

What Are You Doing?

Sternly, with a Bit of Anger
Giant

Words and Music by John Horman

What are you do-ing? What are you do-ing? Here in this gar-den of

mine. Ev'-ry-one out now! With-out a doubt now!

This is my gar-den, all mine. All to my-self now,

I'll keep my gar-den just for me so fine!

Now the children had nowhere to play.
When they walked by the garden, they
remembered how beautiful it had been.

How Happy We Were There

With Sadness *First verse: Children*
Second verse: Chorus

Words and Music by John Horman

do

1. We once were hap - py there. _____
2. The gar - den was their friend. _____

We once were hap - py there. _____
But that is at an end. _____

Each day was filled with friends and fun; ___
So self - ish is the gi - ant, now ___

the gar - den was for ev' - ry - one! ___
With - in the wall they're not al - lowed. ___

We once were hap - py there. _____
They once were hap - py there. _____

We ___ once were hap - py there.
They ___ once were hap - py there.

Since the Giant had been so selfish, Spring decided not to visit the garden. Summer and Fall also refused to warm the garden and give it fruit. So it was always Winter there.

The Arrival of Winter

Words and Music by John Horman

The Selfish Giant wondered why the seasons did not visit the garden.

Spring Has Forgotten

Fairly Fast, with Movement
Snow/Frost/Hail/North Wind

Words and Music by John Horman

Spring has for-got-ten,   for - got-ten this   gar-den.

Now we can live here   all year long.   Warm winds of spring-time,

sweet sum-mer show-ers,   fresh fall fruit won't here be found.

Chorus

Snow   and   Frost   have   both   found   a   home   and

joined by the Hail and the North Wind too. The white cloak of win-ter

re-mains in the gar-den where beau-ti-ful flow-ers and grass-es grew.

One morning the Giant heard some lovely music.

Is That the Sweet Sound?

Slowly, with Feeling
First verse: Giant
Second verse: Chorus

Words and Music by John Horman

1. Is that the sweet sound of mu - sic I hear?
2. Yes, we can hear it so high and so clear.

Roy - al mu - si - cians pass - ing so near?
Could ___ it be ___ that Spring is now here?

Oh what can it be ___ that I ___ have heard?
Yes, Spring ___ has come to us once ___ a - gain.

Can it be? Can it be the sweet sound of a bird?
And the cold-ness of Win - ter has come to an end.

The Giant looked out his window and saw his garden filled with children again. They were sitting in the branches of the trees. Spring had returned! But in one corner of the garden, it was still Winter. A little boy stood crying in the cold.

The Song of the Boy, the Tree, and the Giant

Words and Music by John Horman

Simply, with Tenderness

Boy: I am too small to reach your branch and sit with you, oh
Giant: How ver-y self-ish I have been to keep the chil-dren

tree. __ Bend low so I may touch your bough, from
out. __ Spring comes to those who laugh _ and sing. That's

win-ter we'll be free. *Tree:* I can-not reach you,
what it's all a-bout! *Chorus:* Come take his hand, oh

lit-tle one. You are so ver-y small. _ I wish that
lit-tle one, the win-ter wind will end. __ In-vite the

you could sit _ with me a-mong my branch-es tall.
chil-dren to _ come back, the gar-den lives a-gain!

The frightened children ran away when they saw the Giant. From afar they watched him gently lift the little boy up to the tree.

When the children saw how kind the Selfish Giant had become, they all came back. The Giant decided that his garden would be the children's playground forever!

We're Back in the Garden Again
(to the tune of "How Happy We Are Here")

Children in the Garden

1. We're back in the garden again!
   We're back in the garden again!
   Away with the snow, the wind and the cold.
   The garden is new! Away with the old!
   We're back in the garden again!
   We're back in the garden again!

Chorus and Cast

2. They're back in the garden again!
   They're back in the garden again!
   They love the flowers and the trees.
   Each tiny bird, the warm spring breeze.
   They're back in the garden again!
   They're back in the garden again!

THE TEARS OF THE DRAGON

From a Story by Hirosuke Hamada, English Version by Alvin Tresselt
Words and Music by Teruko Yaginuma
Script Translation from Japanese to English by Christopher Hanzie

In a small village in Japan there once lived a boy
named Akito. He loved to play outdoors with
the other children in the fresh air and sunshine.

KAKURENBO

Words and Music by Teruko Yaginuma
English Version by MMH

Part 1
Child A

Let's play hide and seek, play hide and seek. All come home!

Part 2
Child A

If you touch my fin-ger first then you'll be it for hide and seek.

Part 3
Child A

Part 4
Children

One, two, three! Stone, and pa-per and scis - sors.

Part 5
Children

Part 6
Child B

Pa - per beats a stone. Read - y or not?

Part 7
Children

Part 8
Child B

No, not quite yet. Read - y or not?

Part 9
Children

Part 10
Child B

O K, read - y. I've found you now!

As the children played, they suddenly heard a most frightful sound—a sound they feared more than anything!

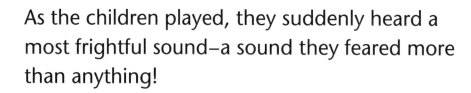

I AM AFRAID

Words and Music by Teruko Yaginuma
English Version by MMH

I am a-fraid!   I am a-fraid!   High on a moun-tain, so

high on the moun-tain top,   There lives a drag-on, soon he will come.

Ter - ri - ble drag-on,   He'll   eat naugh-ty boys and girls.

Ter - ri - ble drag - on,   com-ing for us all!

The frightened children ran away, leaving Akito alone in the dusk. As he thought about the Dragon, he began to wonder if the terrible things he'd heard were really true.

POOR, POOR DRAGON

Words and Music by Teruko Yaginuma
English Version by MMH

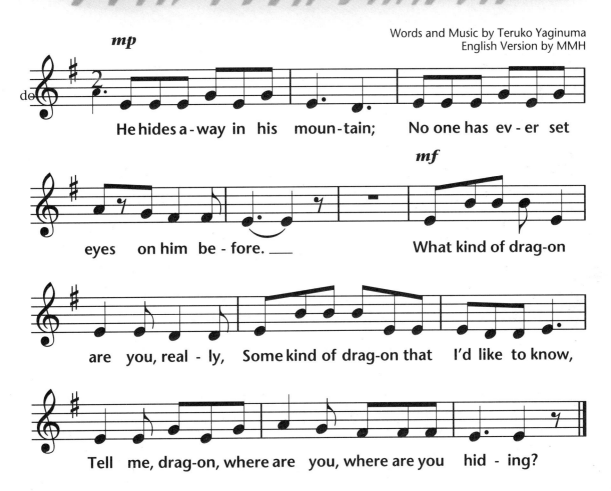

He hides a-way in his moun-tain; No one has ev-er set eyes on him be-fore. ___ What kind of drag-on are you, real-ly, Some kind of drag-on that I'd like to know, Tell me, drag-on, where are you, where are you hid-ing?

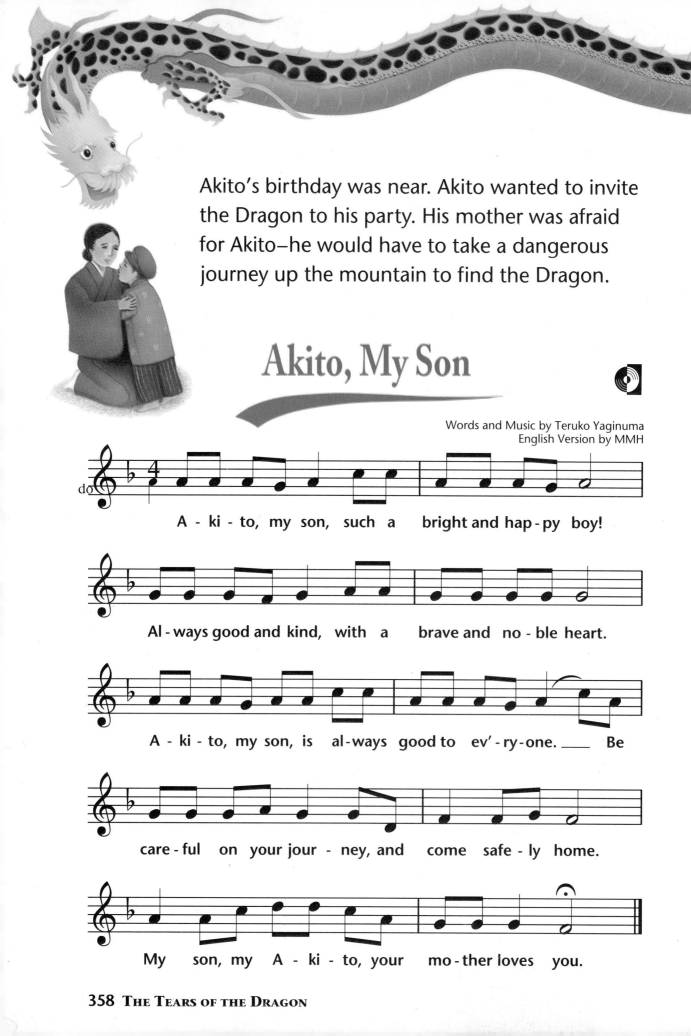

Akito's birthday was near. Akito wanted to invite the Dragon to his party. His mother was afraid for Akito—he would have to take a dangerous journey up the mountain to find the Dragon.

Akito, My Son

Words and Music by Teruko Yaginuma
English Version by MMH

A - ki - to, my son, such a bright and hap - py boy!

Al - ways good and kind, with a brave and no - ble heart.

A - ki - to, my son, is al - ways good to ev' - ry-one. ____ Be

care - ful on your jour - ney, and come safe - ly home.

My son, my A - ki - to, your mo - ther loves you.

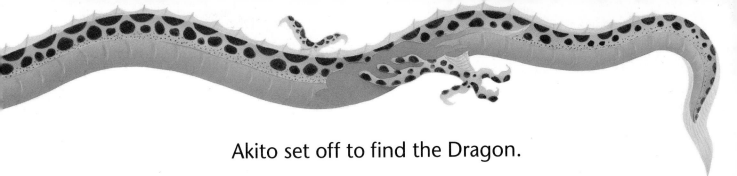

Akito set off to find the Dragon.

LOOKING ~FOR THE~ DRAGON

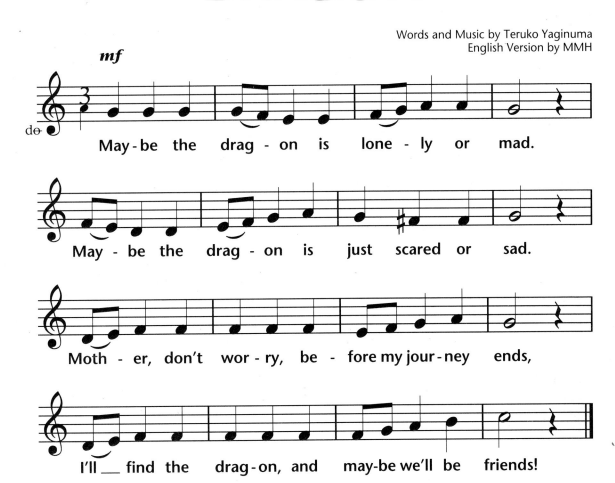

Words and Music by Teruko Yaginuma
English Version by MMH

mf

May - be the drag - on is lone - ly or mad.

May - be the drag - on is just scared or sad.

Moth - er, don't wor - ry, be - fore my jour - ney ends,

I'll __ find the drag - on, and may - be we'll be friends!

Akito climbed to the top of the mountain and began to call for the Dragon.

HELLO, DRAGON

Words and Music by Teruko Yaginuma
English Version by MMH

Akito

Hel - lo, _____ drag-on, _____

Others

Hel - lo, _____ drag-on, _____

End (Fine)

Akito

drag-on. _____ Where are you?

Others

Go back to the beginning and sing to the End.
(Da Capo al Fine)

Where are you? Where are you?

The Dragon was amazed and happy that Akito wanted to be his friend. People had been afraid of him for a long time, and he had been very lonely.

Thank You

Words and Music by Teruko Yaginuma
English Version by MMH

mf

do

Thank you, my friend, thank you, my friend.

Thank you, my friend, for the kind-ness you have shown me.

mp

I am ver-y hap-py you be-lieve in me.

Can it be? Can it be I have a friend?

mf

Thank you, my friend, thank you, my friend.

Warm tears are fall-ing, are fall-ing from my eyes.

The Dragon was so grateful that he began to cry great tears of joy. As the tears fell, they formed a deep river. The Dragon's body turned into a beautiful boat that carried Akito back to his village. Everyone rejoiced to see Akito return safely.

Let's Sing, Everyone

Words and Music by Teruko Yaginuma
English Version by MMH

mf

Group 1 ... **Group 2**

1. Talk, talk-ing ev'-ry-one. Talk, talk-ing ev'-ry-one.
2. Sing, sing-ing ev'-ry-one. Sing, sing-ing ev'-ry-one.

Group 1 ... **Group 2**

Talk, talk to-geth-er. Talk, talk to-geth-er.
Sing, sing to-geth-er. Sing, sing to-geth-er.

Groups 1 and 2

O-pen your hearts and let your ears be in tune, And then

Clap: ... *Stamp:*

ev'-ry-one la la la. Ev'-ry-one la la la.

Here we come in the boat of the drag-on!

GLOSSARY

A

accent (>) a sound that is stronger or louder than the sounds around it, **184**

B

ballet a story that is told through dance and music, **84**

brass family metal instruments such as a trumpet, French horn, trombone, and tuba. They are played by buzzing the lips into the mouthpiece, **194**

C

canon a special kind of imitation. To perform a canon, two or more people begin the same part at different times, **236**

conductor person who leads a musical group, **250**

crescendo (——) to get louder little by little, **98**

D

da capo al fine (D. C. al Fine) Italian words that mean *go back to the start, and keep going until you see the word* Fine, **156**

decrescendo (——) to get softer little by little, **98**

dotted half note (♩.) a musical note that shows a sound that is three beats long, **148**

E

echo a part in music that repeats or copies the part just before it, **178**

eighth notes (♫ or ♪♪) musical notes that show two sounds to a beat, **63**

equal sounds (♫) musical notes that show a trotting rhythm, or two equal sounds to a beat, **187**

F

fine an Italian word that means *the end*, **156**

floor pathway the path your feet make when you move from one place to another. One kind of pathway is a curved pathway, **92**

form the order of sections in music. One musical form is A B form, **141**

forte (*f*) loud, **68**

French horn a higher-pitched instrument in the brass family. Players make sounds by buzzing their lips into the mouthpiece. They play different pitches by pressing different valves, **194**

H

half note (♩) a musical note that shows a sound that is two beats long, **101**

I

imitation when parts of music copy or echo each other, **180**

M

melody several pitches that are sounded one after the other to make a tune. A song has a melody. A speech piece does not have a melody, **114**

N

note a sign for a sound in music, **17**

O

ostinato a musical pattern that repeats over and over, **131**

P

piano (*p*) soft, **68**

pitch the highness or lowness of a sound. Some birds sing on higher pitches. Lions growl on lower pitches, **11**

pitched instruments instruments that sound exact pitches. A piano is a pitched instrument. A hand drum is an unpitched instrument, **88**

Q

quarter note (♩) a musical note that shows one sound to a beat, **63**

quarter rest (𝄽) a musical sign that shows a beat with no sound, **63**

R

repeat sign (:|) a sign that tells you to repeat part of a song, **116**

rest a silence in music, **60**

rhythm long and short sounds and silences that are heard one after the other. You can tap a rhythm on your legs, **18**

rondo a musical form that has different sections. The A section is repeated between each different section. One kind of rondo is A B A C A, **228**

S

staff the lines and spaces on which notes are written, **22**

steady beat the basic unit of time in music. When you can feel the steady beat, you can walk or march to the music, **2**

T

texture the sound made when different pitches, rhythms, and tone colors are played or sung together, **207**

tie (⌣) a musical sign that joins two notes on the same pitch. It tells you to sound the first note and hold it through the second note, **100**

tremolo a longer sound made by playing a pitch over and over very quickly, **119**

trombone a larger and lower-pitched instrument in the brass family. Players make sounds by buzzing their lips into the mouthpiece. They play different pitches by moving the slide in or out, **195**

trumpet the smallest and highest-pitched instrument in the brass family. Players make sounds by buzzing their lips into the mouthpiece. They play different pitches by pressing different valves, **195**

tuba the largest and lowest-pitched instrument in the brass family. Players make sounds by buzzing their lips into the mouthpiece. They play different pitches by pressing different valves, **195**

U

unequal sounds (♩♪) musical notes that show a galloping or skipping rhythm, or two unequal sounds to a beat, **187**

unpitched instruments instruments that do not sound exact pitches. A woodblock is an unpitched instrument. A trumpet is a pitched instrument, **88**

CLASSIFIED INDEX

FOLK MUSIC

INDEX OF LITERATURE

INDEX OF LISTENING SELECTIONS

Index of Songs and Speech Pieces

ACKNOWLEDGMENTS

D.C. Heath & Co. for *A Shepherd Song* from ENJOYING MUSIC—NEW DIMENSIONS IN MUSIC by Robert A. Choate, Richard C. Berg, Lee Kjelson, and Eugene W. Troth. English lyrics by Moshe Jacobson and Eugene W. Troth. Reprinted by permission of D.C. Heath & Co. For *The Wind Song*, words by Cecil Cowdrey, from MUSIC FOR YOUNG AMERICANS, #3. By permission of D.C. Heath & Co.

Holt, Rinehart and Winston, Inc. for *Halloween* by Lynn Olson from EXPLORING MUSIC 2 by Eunice Boardman and Beth Landis, copyright © 1971 by Holt, Rinehart and Winston, Inc., reprinted by permission of the publisher. For *Hey, Mr. Monday* (aka *Mr. Monday*) from EXPLORING MUSIC, Grade 1, by Eunice Boardman and Beth Landis. Copyright © 1975 by Holt, Rinehart and Winston, Inc., adapted by permission of the publisher.

Kaisei-sha and Scholastic, Inc. for *Tears of the Dragon* (idea/story line) by Hirosuke Hamada. Copyright © Kaisei-sha, Tokyo (Japanese). English translation by Alvin Tresselt. Reprinted by permission of Kaisei-sha and Scholastic, Inc.

Bobbi Katz for *Morning Song* from POEMS FOR SMALL FRIENDS by Bobbi Katz, published by Random House, Inc., © 1989. Used by permission of the author.

Kir and Elizabeth Kuklowsky for *Blackie,* Op.1, No. 1, by Kir and Elizabeth Kuklowsky from ACTION SONGS FOR CHILDREN—UKRAINIAN by Kir Kuklowsky. Copyright © Kir Kuklowsky.

Marci Ridlon McGill for *Johnny* from THAT WAS SUMMER by Marci Ridlon McGill. Published by Follett Publishing Co. Copyright © 1969 by Marci Ridlon McGill.

MGA Agency (Macmillan of Canada Ltd.) for *Skyscraper* by Dennis Lee, © Dennis Lee, 1974.

MM Publications for *Tue, Tue.* © Mona Lowe, MM Publications, Yucca Valley, CA.

MMB Music, Inc. for *Pizza, Pizza, Daddy-O* from LET'S SLICE THE ICE by Eleanor Fulton and Pat Smith. © 1978 MMB Music, Inc., Saint Louis. Used by Permission. All Rights Reserved.

Music Educators National Conference for *Mos', Mos'!* collected by David McAllister. Used by permission of Hotteville-Bacavi Community School, Hotteville, AZ. Arrangement from MULTICULTURAL PERSPECTIVES IN MUSIC EDUCATION by William M. Anderson and Patricia Shehan Campbell. © 1989 Music Educators National Conference. Used by permission of MENC.

Music Sales Corporation for *Lenny* and *Mumble Grumble* by Minnie O'Leary from ALL DAY LONG SONGS. Copyright © 1974, 1979 Shawnee Press, Inc. (ASCAP). International Copyright Secured. All Rights Reserved. Used by Permission.

Alice Olsen Publishing Co. for *Tafta Hindi* from MUSICA ARABIA by Alice Olsen. © 1987 Alice Olsen Publishing Co. All rights reserved. Printed in USA.

Oxford University Press for *Chrismus A Come* from BEENY BUD, by permission of Oxford University Press.

Paws IV Publishing Company for *Old bull moose who dreamed he could fly...* by Shelley R. Gill. © 1986 Shelley R. Gill.

Pelican Publishing Company, Inc. for *A Paris*, folk song from CHANTEZ ENCORE by Jeanne and Robert C. Gilmore. Copyright © 1977 by Jeanne and Robert C. Gilmore. Used by permission of the licensor, Pelican Publishing Company, Inc.

Plays, Inc. for *The Wearing of the Green*. Reprinted by permission from HOLIDAY PROGRAMS FOR BOYS AND GIRLS by Aileen Fisher. Copyright © 1989 by Aileen Fisher. Publisher: Plays, Inc., Boston, MA.

Prentice Hall for *When I Am Ten Years Old* from THIS IS MUSIC. © 1967 Allyn & Bacon by permission of Prentice Hall.

Putnam/Grosset for *You'll Find Whenever the New Year Comes*, reprinted by permission of Philomel Books from CHINESE MOTHER GOOSE RHYMES, selected & edited by Robert Wyndham, copyright © 1968 by Robert Wyndham.

Marian Reiner for *An old silent pond* by Harry Behn from CRICKET SONGS: JAPANESE HAIKU TRANSLATED BY HARRY BEHN. Copyright © 1964 Harry Behn. © Renewed 1992 Prescott Behn, Pamela Behn Adam, and Peter Behn. Reprinted by permission of Marian Reiner. For *Toaster Time* from THERE IS NO RHYME FOR SILVER by Eve Merriam. Copyright © 1962, 1990 by Eve Merriam. Reprinted by permission of Marian Reiner for the author. For *Until I Saw the Sea* from I FEEL THE SAME WAY by Lilian Moore. Copyright © 1967 by Lilian Moore. Reprinted by permission of Marian Reiner for the author.

Belle San Miguel-Ortiz for *Que Bonito Es* by Belle San Miguel-Ortiz. Copyright © by Belle San Miguel-Ortiz.

Scholastic, Inc. and Kaisei-sha for *Tears of the Dragon* (idea/story line) by Hirosuke Hamada. Copyright © Kaisei-sha, Tokyo (Japanese). English translation by Alvin Tresselt. Reprinted by permission of Scholastic, Inc. and Kaisei-sha.

Schroder Music Co. for *I Live in a City*. Words & music by Malvina Reynolds; © 1961 Schroder Music Co. Renewed 1989 Nancy Schimmel. Used by permission. All rights reserved.

Charles Scribner's Sons for *The Way to Start a Day*. Reprinted with permission of Charles Scribner's Sons, an imprint of Macmillan Publishing Company, from THE WAY TO START A DAY by Byrd Baylor. Text copyright © 1977, 1976 Byrd Baylor.

Silver, Burdett & Ginn Inc. for *Pick a Pumpkin* by Naomi Caldwell from THE MAGIC OF MUSIC—KINDERGARTEN, © Copyright, 1970, 1965, by Ginn and Company. Used by permission of Silver, Burdett & Ginn Inc. For *When You Send a Valentine*, music by Luella Garrett, from The Kindergarten Book of OUR SINGING WORLD Series, © Copyright 1959, 1957, 1949, by Ginn and Company. Used by permission of Silver, Burdett & Ginn Inc.

The Society of Authors for *Someone* by Walter de la Mare, as the literary representative of the Trustees of Walter de la Mare.

Kathy B. Sorensen for *Lek Kansaing*, collected and transcribed by Kathy Sorensen. © 1991 Kathy B. Sorensen.

Kay Stephens for *Sylvester the Snake* by Kay Stephens. Copyright © Kay Stephens.

Margaret Winsor Stubbs for *Humpty Dumpty sat on a wall* by Frederick Winsor from THE SPACE CHILD'S MOTHER GOOSE by Frederick Winsor and Marian Parry, copyright 1958, 1986 Simon & Schuster.

Charles E. Tuttle Co., Inc., for *The Spider Weaver* from JAPANESE CHILDREN'S FAVORITE STORIES by Florence Sakade. Reprinted by permission of Charles E. Tuttle Co., Inc., of Tokyo, Japan.

Valen Associates for *At the Top of My Voice* by Felice Holman from AT THE TOP OF MY VOICE and other poems, Charles Scribner's Sons, © 1970. Used by permission of the author.

Warner Bros. Publications Inc. for *Chicken Soup with Rice*. Words by MAURICE SENDAK. Music by CAROLE KING. © 1975 COLGEMS-EMI MUSIC INC. & ELORAC MUSIC. All rights controlled and administered by COLGEMS-EMI MUSIC INC. All Rights Reserved. Used by permission.

World Music Press for *Kye Kye Kule* and *Sorida* from LET YOUR VOICE BE HEARD! SONGS FROM GHANA AND ZIMBABWE by Abraham Kobena Adzenyah, Dumisani Maraire, and Judith Cook Tucker. © 1986 Dumisani Maraire/World Music Press, P.O. Box 2565, Danbury, CT 06813. Used by permission. For *La Paloma Se Fué*, as remembered (sung) by Alejandro Jimenez, who grew up in Quebradillas, Puerto Rico. Annotation & Arrangement © 1988 Alejandro Jimenez/World Music Press, P.O. Box 2565, Danbury, CT 06813.

ART & PHOTO CREDITS

COVER DESIGN: Designframe Inc., NYC

COVER PHOTOGRAPHY: Jade Albert for MMSD

Cover Set Design by Mark Gagnon
Trumpet courtesy of Selmer Company Inc.

ILLUSTRATION

Mike Adams, 192-193; Elizabeth Allen, 68-71; Yvette Banek, 174-175; Bill Basso, 246-249; Elliot Bergman, 250-251; Lisa Berrett, 260-261; Alex Bloch, 60-61, 65, 107 (b/w), 130-131, 148, 152-153, 172-173, 194, 200 (top), 206 (inset), 238-239, 240-241 (border), 243 (top), 288-289; Joe Boddy, 178-179; Deborah Borgo, 138-139; Pat Brangle, 94-95, 102-103, 132-133, 220-221; Patrick O. Chapin, 2-3, 38-41, 243-245; Lisa Chauncy Guida 100-101, 198-199, 299 (bottom), 300 (top), 312, 316, 318, 320-322, 325, 331, 333, 337; Randy Chewning, 234-235; Jaimie Collins, 286-287; Gwen Connally, 88-91; Jane Conteh-Morgan, 66-67; Mark Corcoran, 258-259; Donna Corvi, 118-119; Lisa Cypher, 142-143; Don Daily, 210-211; Daniel Del Valle, 97, 156-157; Darius Detweiler, 184-185; Cathy Diefendorf, 0-1; Wendy Edelson, 222-223, 252-253; David Garner, 4-5; Doreen Gay-Kassel, 216-217; Patrick Girouard, 236-237; Jack Graham, 112-113; Gershom Griffith, 282-283, 340-341; John Gurney, 200-201; Annie Gusman, 20-25; Cynthia Fitting, 44-45; Melanie Hall, 46-47; Mark Herman, 146-149; Jean Hiroshima, 168-169, 354-363; Dennis Hockerman, 188-189, 270-273; Joan Holub, 240-241; Catherine Huerta, 140-141; Susan Huls, 80-83; Cynthia Jabar, 50-51; Dave Joly, 34-37; Manuel King, 114-115; Linda La Galia, 86-87, 224-225; Joe Lapinski, 126-127; Al Leiner, 176-177, 292; Katherine Mahoney, 128-129; Claude Martinot, 290-291; David McCall Johnson, 186-187; Frank McShane, 26-27; Patrick Merrell, 14-15, 158-161; David Milgrim, 196-197; Yosie Miyake, 208-209; Leo Monahan, 150-151, 276-277; Marsha Moore, 206-207; Deborah Morse, 296-298, 308, 313, 318, 324, 327, 329, 332, 336; Dave Nehila, 162-165; Lori Nelson Field, 232-233; Jose Ortega, 28-29, 274-275; Cyndi Patrick, 10-11, 294-295, 301, 309, 315, 319, 323, 326, 328, 335, 338-339; Kathy Petrauskas, 106-107; Jean Pidgeon, 120-121; Debbie Pinkney, 264-265; Doug Roy, 202-205; Bob Shein, 58-59; Neil Shigley, 8-9; Robbie Short, 190-191; Mou Sien Tseng, 278-281; Geraldo Suzan, 134-135; Susan Swan, 122-125; Andrea Z. Tachiera, 299 (top), 300 (bottom), 302-306, 311, 332, 334; Mary K. Thelen, 76-77; Gary Torrisi, 226-227; Stan Tusan, 230-231; Fabricio Vanden Broeck, 78-79, 98-99; Joe Veno, 104-105; David Wenzel, 266-267; Josie Yee, 92-93; Lane Yerkes, 54-55, 136-137, 214-215, 262-263, 344-353.

PHOTOGRAPHY

All photographs are by the Macmillan/McGraw-Hill School Division (MMSD) except as noted below.

i: instruments, Jim Powell Studio for MMSD. iv-v: instruments, Jim Powell Studio for MMSD. vi: t.l. instruments, Jim Powell Studio for MMSD. **Unit 1** 6: b.m., l. Ken Karp for MMSD; r. Mark A. Philbrick for MMSD. 7: Culver; b.r. Matthew McVay/Allstock; m.l. Richard Pasley; m.r. Woodfin Camp & Associates, Inc.; t.r. Lawrence Schiller/Photo Researchers, Inc. 8: Mark A. Philbrick for MMSD. 11: Ken Karp for MMSD. 21: Henry Ford Museum, Research Center. *Model T on the Farm,* ca. 1951-52. Norman Rockwell/From the collection of Henry Ford Museum and Greenfield Village O-3967(J)/1325-3. 33: b. *Le Village en Fête* by Miguel Vivancos/Musée National d'Art Moderne, Centre National d'Art et de Culture, George Pompidou; t. *Montezuma's Head/*Anna Hills, courtesy Maxwell Galleries, San Francisco. 35, 36: Ken Karp for MMSD. 37: b.l., m., t.r. Jim Powell Studio for MMSD. 37:

b.r., t.l. Ken Karp for MMSD. 42: Lynn Goldsmith/LGI. 43: Blake Little. **Unit 2** 49: Giraudon/Art Resource. 50-51: David Reed/Panos Pictures. 56: Ken Karp for MMSD. 57: Scribner/Picture Cube; inset, Bonnie Kamin. 59: Ken Karp for MMSD. 60, 61, 62: Ken Karp for MMSD. 63: t. Richard Haynes Jr.; t.r. Ken Karp for MMSD. 64-65: Ken Karp for MMSD. 70: The Bettmann Archive. 72: Palmer C. Hayden Collection, Gift of Miriam A. Hayden, The Museum of African American Art. 74-75: Ian Lloyd/Black Star. 84: l. The Cleveland Ballet/Photo By Richard Termine; r. Herbert Migdoll/Joffrey Ballet. 84-85: Ken Karp for MMSD. 85: b.l. Jack Vartoogian/Joffrey Ballet; b.r. "Ming Hai Wu As Chinese Tea," San Francisco Ballet/Lloyd Englert; t.r. "Waltz Of The Flowers," San Francisco Ballet/Marty Sohl. **Unit 3** 88: b.l., b.r. Jim Powell Studio for MMSD; t.l., t.r. Ken Karp for MMSD. 89: b.m.l., b.r., m., m.r., t.m.r. Jim Powell Studio for MMSD; t.l., t.m.l., t.r. Ken Karp for MMSD. 95: Ken Karp for MMSD. 96: National Gallery, London. 96-97: Luis Castaneda/The Image Bank. 99: Culver Pictures. 105: Edward Christmas. 108-109: b. David Reede; Bruno Bailey/Magnum. 110: b. Charles Mauzy/Allstock; t. Chris Arend/Alaska Stock. 115: Ken Karp for MMSD. **Unit 4** 132-133: bkgnd. Uniphoto. 140: Ann Summa. 144-145: bkgnd. Ken Karp for MMSD. 148-149: bkgnd. Jeff Spielman/Stockphotos. 152: Jim Powell Studio for MMSD. 153: t. Jim Powell Studio for MMSD. 166: b.l. Meridian Arts Ensemble/Peter Schaaf; r. William Waterfall/Stock Market; t.l. Ian Berry/Magnum Photos. 166-167: Frank P. Rossotto/Stock Market. 167: l. Rod Furgason/Unicorn; t.r. Claudia Parks/Stock Market. **Unit 5** 170: b.r. Ken Karp for MMSD; t.l. Ken Karp for MMSD; t.r. Ken Karp for MMSD. 171: b. Ken Karp for MMSD. 172: t. Ken Karp for MMSD. 181: Maxwell Mackenzie/Uniphoto. 182: Metropolitan Museum of Art, Gift of Lila Acheson Wallace, 1983. 194, 195: Ken Karp for MMSD. **Unit 6** 212: b.l. Stephen Frink/Stock Market; b.r. Charles Krebs/Allstock; t. Chuck Bankuti/Shooting Star. 212-213: b. Ken Karp for MMSD. 213: b.r. F. Stuart Wesmorland/Allstock. 218: Albright-Knox Art Gallery, Buffalo, New York. Gift of Seymour H. Knox, 1964. 228: Ken Karp for MMSD. 229: l., r. Ken Karp for MMSD. 234: Ella Jenkins. 240: Greg Christensen/The Image Bank. 241: Weinberg/Clark/The Image Bank. 250: l. Zigy Kaluzny. 251: b. Erich Hartmann/Magnum; t. Richard Bowditch/LGI. **Celebrations** 254-255: Ken Karp for MMSD. 256-257: Regis Lefebure/Stock Broker. 270: Brad Foster/Country Dance and Song Society. 278-279: Mark Stephenson/Westlight. 281: l. Don Klumpp/The Image Bank; r. Terry Madison/The Image Bank. 284-285: Ken Karp. 286-287: Ken Karp for MMSD. 288-289: Travelpix/FPG International. 295: C. Arnesen/Allstock. **Music Library** 340: b. Alexander Doll Company; m.r. Manhattan Doll House; t.l. Library of Congress; t.r. Bridgeman Art Library. 341: b. Courtesy Sam Ash Music; m. Authentic Models; t. Creative Enterprise.

Macmillan/McGraw-Hill School Division thanks The Selmer Company, Inc., and its Ludwig/Musser Industries and Glaesel String Instrument Company subsidiaries for providing all instruments used in MMSD photographs in this music textbook series, with exceptions as follows. MMSD thanks Yamaha Corporation of America for French horn, euphonium, acoustic and electric guitars, soprano, alto, and bass recorders, piano, and vibraphone; MMB Music Inc., St. Louis, MO, for Studio 49 instruments; Rhythm Band Instruments, Fort Worth, TX, for resonator bells; Courtly Instruments, NY, for soprano and tenor recorder; Elderly Instruments, Lansing, MI, for autoharp, dulcimer, hammered dulcimer, mandolin, Celtic harp, whistles, and Andean flute.

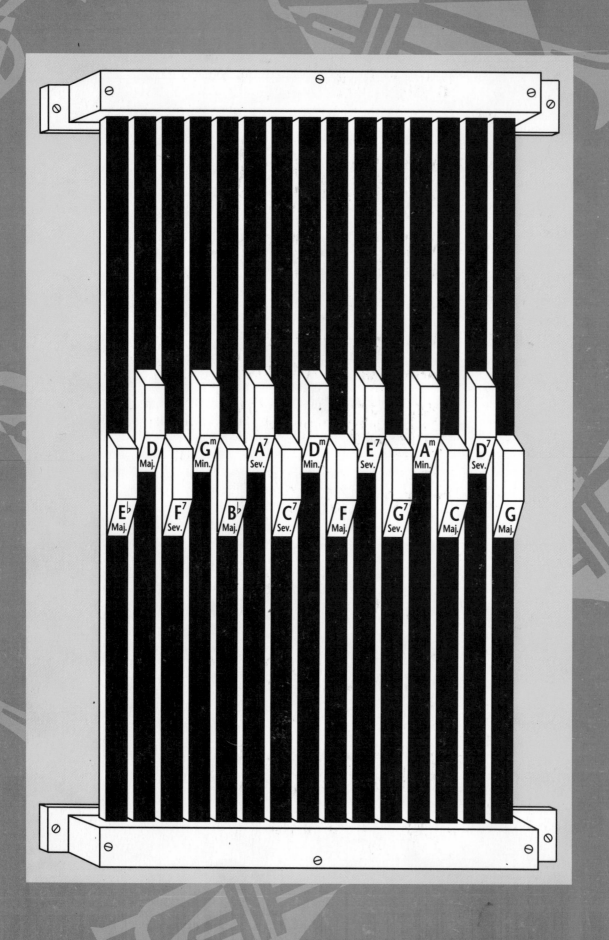